Jesus Christ
AND
CHRISTIAN VISION

Douglas F. Ottati

FORTRESS PRESS   Minneapolis

COPYRIGHT © 1989 BY AUGSBURG FORTRESS

———————

Library of Congress Cataloging-in-Publication Data

Ottati, Douglas F.
Jesus Christ and Christian vision.

1. Jesus Christ—Person and offices.   2. Christian
life—1960–   . I. Title.
BT202.08 1989   232   99–45247
ISBN 0–8006–2316–9

———————

3467J88   Printed in the United States of America   1-2316

FOR C. M. S.

Contents

Preface

The aim of this book is to present a christology of the heart that is informed by the classical Christian heritage and engages contemporary believers. Accordingly, my portrait of the meaning and significance of Jesus Christ emphasizes the importance of affectivity for personal identity. My basic claim is that, in and through his life's dominant devotion, Jesus Christ centers a distinctive vision of God and a distinctive way of life.

A second prominent feature of my interpretation is that it discerns practical significance in what Jesus says, does, and endures. Rather than reduce Jesus of Nazareth to a redemptive event apart from any integral relation to ethics, I try to show that a certain affective pattern, balance, or integrity is communicated to people in Jesus Christ and that this lends their lives a distinctive orientation. For this conviction, I am indebted not only to the longer Christian heritage but also to an American tradition in philosophy and theology that includes figures like Jonathan Edwards, Horace Bushnell, Walter Rauschenbusch, Josiah Royce, Charles Pierce, and H. Richard Niebuhr. Portions of my argument may be read as an attempt to make good on the christological promise of this tradition with the aid of more contemporary ideas about biology, society, and human agency.

My argument is also guided by the conviction that christology probes an originating pattern for the Christian community's orientation in and perspective on the world. Christological reflection inquires into a particular lens or key by which Christians interpret circumstances and realities in their attempt to envision the whole of life in relation to God. In this respect, my approach is friendly to the recent nonfoundationalist turn in contemporary theology with its heightened appreciation for the historical particularity of human knowing. I agree that we do not work from neutral universal insights in theology or in any other reflective enterprise. Like H. Richard Niebuhr, I find epistemological and theological reasons for beginning in Christian theology with the historical tradition of the Christian community.

At the same time, however, it is important to realize that as we attempt to envision the whole of life in relation to God, we interpret circumstances and realities that are interpreted from other perspectives as well. The terms and meanings of our inherited Christian tradition give us our bearings, and they predispose us to see things in certain ways. Yet changing circumstances and realities, as well as alternative interpretations offered from other perspectives, may challenge and enrich our received terms and meanings. They may even lead us to revise them.

For these reasons, I differ from theologians whose exclusive criterion for meaning and truth is fidelity to the internal resources of the Christian community. Indeed, I believe that isolationist stances are flawed on theological grounds, since the central terms of the historical Christian tradition point toward a universal Creator, Governor, and Redeemer. This particular content impels Christians to interpret changing circumstances and realities, and also to assess relationships between the Christian community's perspective and perspectives generated by other, no less particular, communities of inquiry and belief.

These suppositions inform the contents of the chapters that follow. Chapter One sets the christological task in the context of the continuing life of the Christian community. It indicates that a responsible and constructive accounting of what our predecessors have said about Jesus Christ is an interpretative act which attempts to further the orientation and identity of the Christian community in its present environment. The second chapter shows that the classical tradition of the Christian community affirms both the centrality and particularity of Jesus Christ. Interplay between these two affirmations is crucial. Jesus Christ is central for the Christian community's apprehensions of God and human life precisely because these apprehensions receive specific form and content from the particulars of what Jesus Christ says,

does, and endures. Chapter Three recognizes that the interplay between centrality and particularity is rendered problematic by the rise
of critical historical scholarship. I argue, nevertheless, that a critical
reading of the New Testament in light of recent perspectives on human
behavior upholds both the centrality and particularity of Jesus Christ.
The fourth chapter, "The Truth, the Way, and the Life," uses a symbolic shorthand drawn from the church's theological tradition to the-
matize the particulars of what Jesus Christ says, does, and endures.
These particulars express an affectively charged pattern or symbolic
form that shapes the Christian community's vision of God and of
human life in appropriate relation to God. Chapter Five returns to the
affirmation of Christ's centrality. Rather than rely upon the metaphysical language of two natures in one hypostasis, I suggest that the
reality of God and of human life in appropriately responsive relation
to God is mediated in and through the affective balance of what Jesus
says, does, and endures. Finally, if the Christian way is anchored by
the centrality of a particular historic figure and not by evidently universal truths, then the relationship between the Christian way and
other perspectives on life needs to be addressed. This is the subject of
my sixth and concluding chapter.

A number of people and institutions have helped me bring this
project to completion. Union Theological Seminary in Virginia granted me sabbatical leave in 1983–84, during which time I began work
on the manuscript while I was a research fellow in the Center for the
Advanced Study of Religion at the Divinity School of the University
of Chicago. My friend and officemate there, William Warthling,
helped to liven my spirits and sharpen my ideas. Richard Dietrich,
Thomas Are, John Judson, W. Stacy Johnson, Jr., and W. Carter Lester,
Jr.—all of them at one time or another students at Union—read and
commented upon earlier drafts. I am grateful to my friend William
Schweiker for his perceptive remarks, and to my colleague Rebecca
Weaver for conversations about historical sources. I should also like
to thank Michael West, my editor at Fortress Press, for many helpful
suggestions.

I doubt that there is anything I have written over the past ten
years that has not been improved by almost constant conversation
with my colleague at Union, Charles Swezey. I continue to be grateful

for the support of two presidents of Union Seminary, Fred Rogers Stair, Jr., and T. Hartley Hall 4th. Like very many writers who give long hours to their work, I owe a special debt to my family—Pamela, Katie, and Albert.

Perhaps more than most, I owe a considerable debt to my teachers. Ten, and in some cases fifteen, years after leaving their classrooms, I continue to learn from James Luther Adams, Robert F. Evans, Benjamin F. Fisher, Langdon Gilkey, James M. Gustafson, Van A. Harvey, Joseph Sittler, and David Tracy. The inquiry which has finally led to this book began with the preparation of a sermon in April 1984 for Northminster Presbyterian Church in Evanston, Illinois. In the fall of 1985, an adult class at Second Presbyterian Church in Richmond gave me an opportunity to teach six sessions on the topic of this book—an experience from which I benefited greatly. I am grateful also to the ministers from the United States and Canada who attended six lectures on "Jesus Christ and the Christian Way" during a week in July 1986 at the annual conference on "Interpreting the Faith" at Union Theological Seminary in Virginia. Their responses encouraged me to think that my aim is very near their own.

Douglas F. Ottati
Richmond, Virginia

Thomas said to him, "Lord, we do not know where you are going; how can we know the way?" Jesus said to him, "I am the way, and the truth, and the life; no one comes to the Father, but by me. If you had known me, you would have known my Father also; henceforth you know him and have seen him."

(John 14:5-7)

1

What It Means to Stand in a Living Tradition

> Our constant endeavor, day and night, is not just to transmit the tradition faithfully, but also to put it in the form we think will prove best.
>
> —John Calvin

Contemporary christology is in crisis. Some ask whether Christianity is possible without incarnation, others cite an "increasing discomfort with the Christ image even within the church."[1] We read varied interpretations of Christ as liberator and as revolutionary, as wise teacher and as friend, as crucified God and as risen Lord, as the one who brings eternity to earth and as the man who is for the world. Some say that Jesus means freedom, others that he means consent to our limitations. A young Uruguayan claims, "For us, Jesus Christ is Che Guevara."[2] One leading theologian writes, "It seems there are as many images of Christ as there are minds."[3] Another says flatly that traditional christology "has fallen apart in our time."[4]

The character of the current crisis should not be misunderstood. It is not particularly difficult to say what christology is. Christology is talk and reflection about Jesus Christ. It is not especially taxing to identify the aim of christology. The aim is to give an interpretation of the meaning and significance of Jesus Christ. Neither have we suddenly been blinded to its historic importance. Christology has been central to much Christian theology because Jesus Christ is pivotal for a Christian vision of God and humanity's place in God's world. Christology is now in crisis because the great affirmations of classical christological doctrine have become questionable. The result is that Christian theology today often appears to be a historic inquiry that has lost its coherence as well as its traditional bearings.

1

THE CONTEXT OF CHRISTOLOGY

To address this crisis one needs to account for the sense of the classical tradition, its meanings and its dynamic patterns, in a fashion that clarifies how they may yet guide and inform contemporary talk and reflection about Jesus Christ. Before turning to that task, however, it is important to set the work of interpretation in the wider context of the ongoing life of the Christian community. Jesus Christ is the focus of a worshiping and ministering community in the present world. To develop a sustained christology, then, is to propose a contemporary statement of the Christian community's center of meaning. A narrowly traditional christology, which merely repeats the past tradition, does not automatically address the current crisis.

Partly, this is because the horizons of many contemporary Christians have been extended, even as their world has grown small, thanks to travel, mass media, and communications. In their homes, they see and hear reports about poverty in urban ghettos, the plight of the small farmer, the nuclear arms race, anti-apartheid demonstrations, Shi'ite Muslims, moonshots, and the "greenhouse effect." They view television series and read magazines and books about different cultures and about the cosmos, its possible beginnings and endings. In their airports, they see devotees of imported eastern religions, even as the security systems remind them of violent conflicts raging around the globe. They inhabit what Richard R. Niebuhr calls a "radial world," in which a global nervous system transmits images, messages, perspectives, ideas, and passions from people and places well beyond the bounds of any local horizon.[5] They are struck by the galaxy of human creeds, the tremendous power and risks of new technologies, recent advances in scientific knowledge, and the enormity of the universe. They are Christians who are curious about and interested in the world, and who seem unwilling and unable to leave their social and cultural premises at the doors of the sanctuary when they assemble to worship. Indeed, they value the experience of interacting with the world. They tend inevitably to evaluate their churches and theologies in light of other interpretations of life, and to evaluate the perspectives presented by their culture in light of their theologies.[6]

For these people, christology is in crisis. In an age that values empirical inquiry more than metaphysics, they are unsure what it means to say that Jesus Christ is truly human and truly divine. In a culture that is only dimly aware of any human fault, they are uncertain what it means to say that Jesus Christ is the redeemer who has won the decisive victory over the forces of sin and darkness. In a society that is often suspicious of large institutions, they are also confused over what official pronouncements have to do with the New Testament and Jesus of Nazareth. Because the great affirmations of classical christology have become questionable, many Christians are perplexed as to whether and how these affirmations may yet guide and inform Christian life and piety in the contemporary world. No mere repetition of past phrases and formulas will adequately address their perplexity.

More profoundly, perhaps, given the inherent dynamic of a living tradition, there is a sense in which a narrowly traditional christology hardly seems possible. A living tradition is a primary source for a community's distinctive identity. It is the "story" of community transmitted for reappropriation in each generation by means of varied artifacts (e.g., texts, art, music, buildings) and activities (e.g., ceremony, commentary, moral behavior). A living tradition shapes present life by furnishing a common memory or heritage that, in turn, yields a guiding orientation.

Let me illustrate. Some time ago, the legislature of the state of New Jersey required that every student in its public high schools take at least two years of courses in American history to graduate. The point of these courses was not to produce a new generation of critical historians but to contribute to the vital transmission of the story of the American nation. Exposure to interpreted documents, monuments, and historical sites sought to ensure that the common memory or heritage of the national community would continue to inform the civic behavior of another generation of Americans, people with names like Smith, Javna, Iwahashi, and Hajinlian. The classes did not exclusively concern the past; they also included attention to current events. The vitalization of a living tradition was reinforced by student government associations and Young Enterprisers' Clubs, as well as by civic rituals on Memorial Day and the Fourth of July.

As any taxpayer will recognize, this process was expensive. The cost was justified by the fact that traditions may be living or dead, and once they have died, they are not easily revived. The vitality of a community depends upon the continuing viability of its tradition. If Smith and Iwahashi do not learn the story and extend its meanings to illumine the challenges and realities of their own experiences, then the distinctive orientation of the American political community is threatened. When the tradition ceases to be reappropriated and extended, the characteristic orientation of the community dies. Traditional artifacts are not destroyed, but they are rendered mute. The interpretative activities by means of which they spoke and were invested with the power to motivate and guide cease. What dies is the vital commitment and willingness of persons to be shaped by the heritage in question and to carry it further in their own time and place. A living tradition enters into the constitution of meaningful life because, by persistent questioning and interpretation, it continues to yield an orientation that makes sense of the continuing experiences of a society of persons. Therefore, to write a sustained christology is to take up the eminently practical task of interpreting and re-presenting the living orientation of the historical Christian community.

Yet not every portion of a heritage carries the same weight or significance.[7] Traditions have varied topographies. They contain high points and low points, peaks, valleys, and plains. So, for example, among participants in the life of the American nation, the presidency of John Tyler is generally thought to have less significance than the presidencies of Abraham Lincoln or Franklin D. Roosevelt. A living tradition contains classic expressions and less compelling ones, and it is part of the work of interpretation to discern which are which.

A classical tradition is that set of expressions that gives seminal representation to the essential characteristics of the community's distinctive orientation or stance. It is constituted by representations that emerge from community-forming figures and events, such as Thomas Jefferson and the Declaration of Independence. A classical tradition both embodies and points toward a cause or an object of devotion, for example, democracy. Its constitutive expressions become the classic originals to which subsequent interpretations must refer. Otherwise, the later interpretations make no genuine claim to furthering the distinctive orientation of the particular community in question. Subsequent interpretations do not simply repeat the originals. If genuine, they stand as creative developments that draw out and extend the fuller meanings of the originals to engage the distinctive challenges and realities of another time. Moreover, a genuinely creative development that truly engages the realities of a subsequent time and place cannot simply be read back into the field of older expressions.

If a subsequent interpretation succeeds at a critical turn in the community's history, it too becomes a benchmark for the interpretations that follow. For example, Lincoln's Emancipation Proclamation and the Nineteenth Amendment to the Constitution of the United States are regarded as compelling developments of the original cause of democracy embodied by Jefferson's Declaration and its revolutionary notion that "all men are created equal"—this despite the fact that Jefferson owned slaves and the Nineteenth Amendment gives *women* the right to vote. Lincoln's Proclamation and the Nineteenth Amendment have taken their places as compelling developments of the essential characteristics of the American political community's identity and orientation. As truly creative developments, they cannot be retroactively translated into the language of Jefferson's Declaration. Nevertheless, no contemporary interpretation of the distinctive identity of the American political community is complete without reference to the compelling meanings of these later documents.

To stand in a living tradition, then, is to participate in a dynamic process of interpretation—one that moves between received heritage and the realities and challenges of the present world in order to express a continuing and vital orientation or identity. The classics remain the criteria for subsequent developments even as their continuing vitality—and the continuing vitality of the entire tradition—depends upon the continuing success of subsequent developments. The classic originals retain a privileged position. There must be a historical chain of connection between them and all subsequent expressions. Nevertheless, subsequent interpretations do not repeat the originals. Indeed, literal repetition often loses a community's distinctive orientation because, in another time and place, the originals do not carry precisely the same meanings that they did in the foundational period. A contemporary interpretation must do no more and no less than engage the community's experiences of the distinctive realities of the present, yet stand in a meaningful measure of continuity with the originals and the subsequent expressions determined to be classical.

The interpretative task is complicated further when the original expressions are multifaceted and contain a number of polarities or tensions that subsequently have been drawn out and resolved in a variety of ways. For example, the originating expressions of the American political community appear to contain a tension between individual liberty and corporate responsibility. This polarity seems to have been resolved differently during the "New Deal" than under the administration of Calvin Coolidge. An inherently dynamic and tensive set of original expressions enables a living tradition to adapt to diverse circumstances—now emphasizing one element or dimension and now another, occasionally spawning new elements and combinations. However, this also means that the interpreter is faced with originating classics that have given rise to differing and sometimes conflicting further developments.

The originating classics of the Christian movement are multifaceted. They include a number of variations on particulars of faith and practice. For example, different titles and images are ascribed to Jesus Christ, and there are differently nuanced statements about divorce. They also contain a variety of general polarities or tensions between knowledge gained from the distinctive heritage of the believing community and from other sources, between the propensities of created nature and the regenerating effects of grace, between sin and the powers of goodness, between law and gospel, and between church and world.[8] Subsequent interpreters draw out these polarities and resolve them in a variety of ways. Thomas Aquinas's interpretation of the tension between nature and grace differs from Martin Luther's. Neither Aquinas nor Luther understand the relation between law and gospel in a way that accords with the more radical ethic of discipleship exposited by the Hutterite, Peter Ridemann, and so on. Then too, none of these three figures simply repeats one or another biblical understanding of law, and it would be unfair to Luther, for example, were one to assume that his interpretation of moral law either can or should be translatable without remainder into Pauline terms. Still, each of these subsequent interpretations stands in some measure of continuity with the multifaceted and tensive originals, and each has been accepted as classic by differing strands within the wider Christian movement. Moreover, even within these differing strands, significant variations occur with respect both to particulars of faith and practice and the general polarities. Within the Reformed strand, for example, Ulrich Zwingli and John Calvin maintain different understandings of the Lord's Supper; Emil Brunner resolves the tension between law and gospel differently than Calvin; and Karl Barth delivers a more negative judgment upon natural theology than any of his Reformed predecessors.

In the face of divergent developments, no single self-consistent interpretation of the distinctive orientation of the Christian movement can stand in unbroken continuity with all that has gone before. Even within specific strands of the wider Christian movement, one must be prepared to tolerate a legitimate (although not an unqualified) plurality of interpretations. This, of course, does not mean that the interpreter is released from the responsibility of showing how his or her work stands in meaningful continuity with some construction of the originals and with at least some of the subsequent expressions accepted as classical. It does mean that the most one can accomplish is a contemporary statement that engages the distinctive realities and challenges of the present age and that stands in a measure of continuity with selected themes presented in the originals and selected subsequent expressions. No self-consistent Christian theology responsibly can claim to comprehend the totality of the historical Christian movement and its varied and multifaceted traditional expressions. To stand in the living tradition of the Christian community, then, means not only to attend to what one has received in its original and subsequent expressions, and not only to attend to present challenges and resources, but also to select constructively from the totality of the historical tradition those themes and strands that seem best.

There is an unavoidably subjective element in any self-consistent theological interpretation. There can be no substitute for the interpreter's personal study of the widest possible cross-section of the historical Christian movement. Neither can there be a substitute for the interpreter's personal appropriation of the distinctive orientation of the Christian movement within the living context of the Christian community. He or she therefore will prize both the cloud of witnesses from other times and places available in books and libraries, and close relationships with present Christian congregations, for these provide critical avenues toward one's own judgments about the distinctive past, vital present, and beckoning future of the Christian movement. They comprise transsubjective checks, which may help to remove the one-sided prejudices and superficialities of initial impressions.

Nevertheless, one's final interpretation of the distinctive orientation or pattern must be offered personally. It is no longer merely a disciplined judgment about the past, but also a constructive act aimed at the present and future. To stand within the living tradition of the Christian community is to take the responsibility of shaping afresh the distinctive orientation of the Christian movement—of defining it anew for a given time and place. The interpreter labors to clarify the continuity that obtains between a contemporary interpretation and the varied historical expressions of the community's distinctive orientation. At the same time, he or she also seeks to shape the living reality for the present. Thus, a contemporary statement of the community's distinctive orientation cannot simply be identified with any one of its past expressions. Neither can it be fairly translated back into the language of previous historical expressions.

Such, then, is the mélange of disciplined and constructive judgments by which one enters the interpretative process that seeks to further the distinctive orientation of the historical Christian community. A living tradition "is the occasion for thought; and precisely because it is something mobile, it requires to be transmitted, not passively or mechanically, but by a conscious, creative act."[9] Those who believe it to be the office of theology to instill absolute certainty are likely to remain dissatisfied with this, since nowhere does the process promise complete assurance as to the truth or correctness of an interpretation. Yet such an assurance seems unavailable as soon as we honestly face the multiplicity and dynamism of the historical Christian movement and the conditioned limitations of our own judgments and aims. What does seem possible, however, is a reasonable confidence that one's careful interpretation of the historical tradition falls within a plausible range of legitimate outgrowths of the originals, and that one's theology makes a credible effort to engage the distinctive challenges and realities of the community's present and foreseeable future. One's labors may contribute to the vital identity of an ongoing community precisely because one dares to risk a constructive statement of a historical orientation for present life.[10]

RECURRENT CHALLENGES

From time to time, the vital power of a tradition may become faint or even fall into disrepute. The past inheritance is thought to be untenable, an irksome burden to be escaped.[11] Then the creative process of interpretation that we have been discussing may be cut short by occasionalist, individualist, and utopian alternatives.[12]

Occasionalists, by concentrating on the reality of the present, overlook both the past and the future. The present consumes past and future. In its most radical forms, occasionalism regards tradition as nothing more than an archaic survival. Rather than consult a received heritage, the occasionalist tries to construct identity exclusively from a reading of present circumstances. The truth in occasionalism is that the present identities of individuals and groups are never forged on the basis of the past alone. At times, therefore, occasionalism may furnish a needed corrective to an uncritical reliance upon a received tradition. It may mount a challenge to entrenched, static, and one-sided interpretations of what we have received, which fail genuinely to risk engaging the distinctive challenges and insights of the present situation.

Nevertheless, occasionalism does not see that the past is unavoidably a part of the present. It fails to recognize that present institutions, values, and behavior are always indissolubly intertwined with a particular past, its material objects, beliefs, images of persons and events, practices, and institutions. Indeed, it fails to comprehend that our perspectives on the present environment and what is at stake in it are partly shaped by the stories of our communities. When it comes to ordering the lives of our families, for example, we cannot escape the orienting power of our responses to our parents, our ancestors, and to the historic ethos of our wider society. Again, it took more than reasoned argument about the contemporary situation of American society to alter the attitudes of many Americans toward certain racial and ethnic minorities. For many American citizens, Martin Luther King, Jr.'s appeals to the classic expressions of the American political community were among his most effective rhetorical strategies. In part, King would say, "Look, by the oppression of black people in this society we fail to live up to the best of our own historical tradition. We fail genuinely to appropriate and develop our true historical identity." The principal value of occasionalism with respect to forming personal and communal identity is that it insists upon the significance of the contemporary situation. In conjunction with received patterns and values, a judicious and critical estimate of the present environment's distinctive features makes a needed contribution to present identity.

Isolated individualism, by concentrating on the self to the exclusion of others, overlooks the common meanings of past, present, and future. It represents the disintegration of community. In its radical form, it regards tradition as a collectivist mold that threatens to suffocate personal vitality. Rather than work with a received heritage, then, individualism tries to forge identity from individual choice and decision alone. Its slogans will approximate "Decide who you shall be" or "You can choose who you will be." The truth in individualism is that identity is never formed apart from personal responses to what has been given to us, to our present possibilities, and to our aspirations for the future. At times, therefore, individualism may counterbalance oppressive and authoritarian interpretations of common identity that foreclose or limit inappropriately our personally creative responses.

Nevertheless, isolated individualism fails to see that the past is not necessarily a collective threat to personality. It fails to see that the past is an inevitable companion of choosing and deciding subjects. It fails to recognize that the orientations of choosing and deciding individuals are inevitably shaped by timely encounters with other people, the longer histories of their social groups, their participation in institutions, customs, morals, and so on. When a young man rebels against his parents or his home town, for example, he rebels in response to his history with his family and the continuing ethos of his immediate surrounding community. His identity may take on the characteristics of a counter-identity, but he is still identified in part by that which he rejects. The principal value of individualism for identity is that it seeks to protect the integrity of personal creativity. An integral individuality that operates creatively in conjunction with received patterns and values in the context of the present environment makes an indispensable contribution to present identity.

Idealistic utopianism, by concentrating on the reality of the future, overlooks both the past and the present. This is its strength and its weakness. Utopianism is a strategy of revolutionary change which, in its most radical forms, regards received tradition as a burden to be overcome. Rather than working within the given tradition, it tries to redirect present identity by constructing an imaginative vision of a changed future. The truth in utopianism is that the present identity of individuals and groups is never forged without reference to an anticipated future, and the future is never a simple extension of the past and the present. Therefore, there are times and situations when utopianism functions as a needed corrective to interpretations of common or individual identity that do not genuinely engage a vision of future possibilities.

Nevertheless, utopianism fails to see that present identity is always responsive to the past as well as to the challenges and realities of the present. Even after revolutionary political change has taken place, the identity of a community does not escape the orienting influences of its prerevolutionary past, nor does the community effectively understand itself apart from the distinctive features of the present. For example, communist China is not only shaped by its responses to the rich and varied heritage of Chinese culture but also by the present realities of international relations and by domestic challenges. Because the present orientation of a community is always formed partly by past and present circumstances, utopianism alone never successfully constitutes present identity. Still, no vital identity is possible without attention to some vision of an anticipated future in conjunction with a received heritage and an interpretation of the present environment.

Partly in response to the acids of occasionalism, individualism, and utopianism, a traditionalism may emerge that regards the distinctive challenges of the present, the creative responses of individuals, and visions of a changed future as threats to be avoided. In its extreme forms, traditionalism attempts to construct present identity entirely out of the past. The truth in this is precisely that the present identities of individuals and groups are never fabricated *de novo*. Therefore, at times when a tradition weakens or falls into disrepute, traditionalism may at least uphold the sense that present identity necessarily is connected with a common heritage.

Nevertheless, traditionalism fails to see that interpretations of present circumstances, personally creative acts, and visions of future possibilities always play a part in the constitution of present identity. It fails to recognize that historic institutions, beliefs, values, and behavior inevitably are shaped by creative responses to present realities and future aspirations. Traditionalistic attempts merely to repeat a past heritage come to grief for at least two reasons. First, the traditionalist is by no means absolved of the necessity of selecting certain themes and expressions from the longer tradition as being especially compelling or classic representations of the historical community's distinctive orientation. Such selections, however, almost always betray some reading or estimate of the distinctive challenges facing the community's present life as well as its future possibilities. Consciously or unconsciously, traditionalistic stances tend to import interpretations of contemporary circumstances and visions of the future into the larger effort to shape the community's present identity. Second, due to the shifting circumstances of history, the past expressions of a given tradition, when repeated in the present, almost never carry the same meanings they had in their original situations. To repeat is to innovate. For example, a decision to repeat Lincoln's Gettysburg Address as a particularly compelling expression of the orientation of the American national community implies the prior judgment that this document, rather than some other, is classic. The mere repetition of Lincoln's address will likely carry different meanings today, given the different challenges and aspirations that now presumably engage "government of the people, by the people and for the people." Moreover, any effort to specify these challenges and aspirations in effect will develop the present meaning of the address, by an interpretation of present circumstances and future possibilities, in directions that Lincoln and his hearers could not have anticipated. Similar things might be said about any mere repetition of the slogan "one man, one vote" in our present environment. Traditionalism fails genuinely to interpret and reappropriate the heritage anew because it trades the dynamic reality of a living community for a static blueprint. It exchanges a living tradition for a dead one, and this is why it often provokes occasionalistic, individualistic, and utopian replies.

To stand in a living tradition is to participate in a community that is consciously informed by its common memory, actively engaged in the realities of the present, vitally concerned about its future direction, and genuinely responsive to personally creative acts of appropriation. It is to acknowledge that the identities of individuals and groups are formed in creative responses to past, present, and future. In short, it is to recognize that a historical tradition, although indispensable, is not an exclusive source for a community's present identity. Vital contributions are made by other resources as well.

RESOURCES FOR THE IDENTITY
OF THE CHRISTIAN COMMUNITY

This last statement especially applies to the Christian community because its historical tradition and christological center point toward the God who is an active power and universal presence. The distinctive orientation of this community is tied to an apprehension of the living Lord whose dominion includes all things in nature and in history, past, present, and future. Given this perception of God in relation to humanity and the world, there can be no exclusive inquiry into the distinctive orientation of the Christian community that eliminates things other than the historical Christian tradition from consideration. To inquire about God from the perspective of the Christian community's historical tradition is always to inquire about other things in our experience and the varied ways in which they may be understood. Continued engagement in the world is mandated by the Christian community's historical perception of God. What is presently known about anything in nature, history, and society is at least potentially relevant for understanding God's purposes and the orientation in human life that coheres with them.

This would not be so if the historic tradition of the Christian community had a limited reality as its cherished object of devotion— if, for example, it had in view a limited lord of the seas or the reality of the human race. Then the field of experiences that might count for or against one's understanding of the object of devotion and its purposes would be less than universal. One or another aspect of nature or history might then be left out of account because it would not count in relation to the cherished object. Yet the cherished object, in relation to which the Christian community dares to say that we live and move and have our being, is no limited reality. For Christians, no corner of nature or history is of no account in relation to God and God's purposes. To be faithful to the theological integrity of *this* particular orientation and identity, Christians must interpret it intelligibly in light of what is currently known about the world from other sources of insight.[13]

There are multiple reference points for present identity within the historical Christian community.[14] Scripture, or the classic literary expressions of the initial stages of the community's life, is most distinctive because it constitutes the original and seminal expression of the orientation of the Christian movement. The closing of the canon stabilizes this resource and makes it the charter document of historical Christian identity.[15] Subsequent expressions of the community whose life is informed by this charter document constitute an emerging and developing tradition, which may be grouped as a second reference point under the rubric of church history. Finally, other resources include the culture in which members of the Christian community participate (e.g., the arts, sciences, philosophy) and the common sense or experiential wisdom of day-to-day life.[16]

A continuing intellectual task of the Christian community is to bring these diverse resources and their varied perspectives into a conversation that maintains meaningful continuity with the distinctive features of its historical tradition. While there is a predisposition toward the confirmation of traditional meanings, this conversation cannot accord equal weight to all of the varied and sometimes conflicting insights of scripture and church history. Instead, it necessarily involves a selective retrieval of certain themes and expressions regarded as classical, giving reasons for how one works with the traditional resources and for the selections that are made. It also entails a critical appraisal of varied and sometimes conflicting insights proffered by the arts, sciences, philosophy, and common sense.

To interpret Jesus Christ as the focused representation of the guiding orientation for the Christian community's present identity requires that one attend to each aspect of this mutually correcting conversation. One needs to show how a contemporary interpretation stands in meaningful continuity with selected scriptural themes and subsequent classical expressions. Again, one needs to weigh the diverse

insights of the arts, sciences, philosophy, and common sense to dis-
cover whether and how they may contribute to a vital contemporary
christology. Here, too, one personally must offer one's contemporary
statement for the critical appraisal of the wider community, knowing
that it is not the only statement possible.

2

Interpreting the Classical Tradition

[T]he sailor who seeks to find his bearings by consulting the charts his fathers used when they set out on the voyage he is continuing, by noting all the corrections they have made upon them and by looking for the stars which gave them orientation may claim at least that he is trying to be true to the meaning of the voyage.
—H. Richard Niebuhr

Our current perplexity in making sense christologically is heightened by the considerable diversity within the New Testament itself. I once had a teacher in divinity school who said that there are in the New Testament something on the order of thirteen to seventeen different christologies. Some present Jesus as God's Son, while others identify him with a heavenly figure called the Son of man. Some portray Jesus as the second Adam, while others regard him as God's wisdom. Still others depict Jesus Christ as God's Logos or preexistent Word. For our purposes, the more important point is not just how many different christologies one may identify within the canon, but rather that recent scholarship has made us increasingly aware of the theological richness of the New Testament portraits of Jesus. This, in turn, has complicated the question of the unity of New Testament christology. Matthew, Mark, Luke, John, Paul—each offers relatively distinct views of Jesus and his significance. When we look to the New Testament, we do not find a single christology but a variety of christologies, which turn upon a multiplicity of images, metaphors, and symbols. For this reason, it is no longer readily apparent just how one may frame an interpretation of Jesus Christ that stands in meaningful continuity with the New Testament witnesses.

If, however, we can no longer underestimate the christological diversity of the New Testament, neither should we overestimate it. There appears to be general agreement among New Testament writers on two related points. The first is that Jesus Christ is central and decisive for God's converse with us. This seems obvious enough as soon as we observe that what is collected in the New Testament is not a single book, but rather a small library of early Christian literature. And, unlike the larger library of the Hebrew scriptures, most of the volumes in this smaller collection struggle with the meaning and significance of a single figure. More importantly, perhaps, to say that Jesus is the Christ is to assert his decisiveness for God's converse with us. For "the Christ" is not a surname like "Jones" or "Smith," but a title something like "apostle," "king," or "Mr. President." This comes through in the ancient expression "Christ Jesus," which Paul uses in his letters. To say "Christ Jesus" is something like saying "the apostle Paul" or "King David" or "President Lincoln." It is to identify Jesus with a specific title. "Christ" is the title of God's anointed one who stands in a special relationship with God and God's people. The Christ is the messiah, the one who proclaims the advent of God's kingdom and in whom that kingdom is made manifest. He is, in the words of the popular hymn, the long-awaited Emmanuel who has come to ransom captive Israel. He is the one whom we may follow and thus become disciples of God's way with the world. He is decisive for our apprehension of God and God's purposes as well as for our apprehension of who we are in relation to God. Without the Christ, we do not truly apprehend God and God's purposes, nor do we understand who we ourselves truly are. To say that Jesus is the Christ is to assert that in him we have the decisive embodiment of God's grace, purposes, and power, and in him we have a paradigm for our relation to God. This I take to mean that, in some fundamental sense, our experience of Jesus Christ is, at one and the same time, experience both of the reality of God and of human life in appropriate relation to God. In this way, *the New Testament affirms the centrality of Jesus Christ.*

A second broad area of agreement is that a correct perception of what Jesus of Nazareth says, does, and endures is critically important for a correct understanding of the Christ. We cannot know the Christ simply by knowing that he is an expected savior or messiah. We also

must attend to the specifics of Jesus' life, ministry, death, and resurrection. This comes through somewhat in kerygmatic summaries
such as the one in 1 Corinthians 15, and it is essential to Paul's claim
that we preach "Christ crucified." It also gives us insight into why
the early Christian communities should have produced gospels in the
first place. Why not simply announce that the Christ has come? Why
take the time to tell the whole story of this man Jesus? Because the
Christ is this particular man, who said and did particular sorts of
things, who was despised, rejected, and killed, and who rose again.
Jesus of Nazareth, the one who proclaimed a message of repentance
and God's kingdom, who associated with tax collectors and sinners,
and who was persecuted, defines "the Christ" every bit as much as
"the Christ" defines Jesus of Nazareth. Therefore, our experience of
God and of human life in appropriately responsive relation to God is
applied specifically to the life, ministry, death, and resurrection of this
particular man. If we do not know that the Christ is this particular
person, Jesus of Nazareth, then we do not really know what God
requires and who we ourselves truly are. The New Testament insists
that the contours of God's grace, purposes, and power, as well as the
contours of our relation to God, be applied specifically to this particular
figure. In this sense, *the New Testament affirms the particularity of Jesus
Christ.*[1]

Thus, with respect to construals of the significance of Jesus Christ
in the New Testament, we do not have harmony, although we do
have both unity and diversity. There are two basic points of agreement,
yet just how these points are imaged or thematized differs from author
to author and even within the writing(s) of a single author. One implication of this observation is that a single, self-consistent christology
cannot repeat all that the New Testament says about Jesus Christ. No
single christology can reproduce or replace the New Testament witnesses, and the New Testament continues to function as a fund of
images and conceptualities that may be employed to help specify the
significance of Jesus Christ for Christian faith and life. (This, inci-
dentally, is one of the reasons why it is most important to hand on
to each succeeding generation the Bible and not just one or another
theological treatise!) But it must also be recognized that, relative to

the whole field of New Testament possibilities, particular self-consistent christologies are necessarily selective in their emphases and thematizations. We should therefore admit a legitimate, although not unqualified, measure of plurality in Christian views of Jesus Christ that stand in meaningful continuity with the New Testament witnesses. This admission is based upon the New Testament itself:

> [F]rcm the first the significance of Christ could only be apprehended by a diversity of formulations which though not always strictly compatible with each other were not regarded as rendering each other invalid . . . it would be unwise to attempt to hold all the diverse formulations in play at the same time, and unpractical to insist on the equal validity of each in every circumstance. As Schillebeeckx rightly notes: "A thoroughly scriptural orthodoxy does not entail conferring upon Jesus simultaneously all of the images and titles available."[2]

From these observations, it is a short step to another that is critical for an understanding of the early development of christological doctrine: The classical creeds and formulas of the Hellenistic church cannot repeat *the* christology of the New Testament. Indeed, as I will argue, they do not repeat any particular christology within the New Testament. Nevertheless, the really important question is not whether the classical creeds and formulas repeat the New Testament, but whether and in what senses they may be said to stand in meaningful continuity with the theologically diverse literature we find there.

My purpose in what follows is to show how the classical tradition may inform contemporary talk and reflection about Jesus Christ. Accordingly, I interpret developments in christology proceeding through some of the early local creeds, the Council at Nicea in 325, and the Council at Chalcedon in 451. I also interpret the contributions of Protestant reformers and theologians during the nineteenth and twentieth centuries. I suggest that the extracanonical development of christological doctrine upholds both the centrality and the particularity of Jesus Christ. This is the major thread of continuity that runs through the ages. The early local creeds intimate both points. Nicea and Chalcedon sharpen the affirmation of Christ's centrality under the distinctive pressures of Hellenistic culture and imperial Roman politics. Protestant reformers, partly due to their heightened interest in atonement, contribute important symbolizations of the particulars of what Jesus Christ says, does, and endures. Nevertheless, the overall development of classical christology is dynamic. At no point can we say that its main contributors either simply or unquestioningly repeat what they have received. Moreover, in light of fundamental criticisms made during the nineteenth and twentieth centuries, it is apparent that the classical tradition accumulates a number of problems for christology which were not adequately resolved. A basic issue for contemporary reflection, then, is how to articulate both the centrality and the particularity of Jesus Christ without being shackled by the problematic terms and conceptualities of our forebears.

CENTRALITY AND PARTICULARITY
IN THE LOCAL CREEDS

Many of the key phrases of classical christology—the Son is "of the same essence as the Father," in Christ's "one person" are "two natures" without separation or confusion—now give the impression that the early creeds are products of an entirely speculative enterprise. This is not so. Up until the beginning of the fourth century, it was the day-to-day life of local congregations, in worship, preaching, baptism, catechetical instruction, and written correspondence, that supplied occasions for the development of creedal statements. For example, the text that has come down to us as the Apostles' Creed was originally used by the church at Rome as a baptismal formula. A previous version, sometime during the second century, probably looked like this:

> I believe in God the Father Almighty, and in Christ Jesus, his son, our Lord, and in the Holy Spirit, the holy church, the forgiveness of sins, the resurrection of flesh.[3]

This statement, whose structure resembles the baptismal command in Matt. 28:19, presents an early summary of Christian beliefs and affords a glimpse of the church's early christology in the west. It clearly expresses Jesus' vital relationship to "God the Father Almighty." For the second-century catechumen, the term "Father" carried the meaning of the compassionate one of the Lord's Prayer who is at the same time the source of the universe. Indeed, the Greek word translated by the

English "Almighty" is *pantokrator,* and more properly means "all-governing" or "all-ruling." The phrase "in Christ Jesus, his son, our Lord" applies three biblically attested titles to Jesus. That Jesus is God's Son repeats a favorite claim of the New Testament; the all-governing Father of the universe is also the Father of Christ Jesus. The formula "Christ Jesus" indicates that, in the early Roman church, "Christ" was not yet a proper name but remained a title equivalent to the Hebrew "messiah." "Lord" was also a typical element in Christian teaching, preaching, and confession from the first. Here, it appears to emphasize the interrelation between Jesus' divine sonship and his significance for us. Christ Jesus, the Son of the all-governing Father, is also our Lord, an appropriate object of worship and devotion.[4]

Later additions may be understood in connection with needs and occasions that led to the creed's expansion. The word "only" (*monogenes, unicus*), which now appears before "son," is almost certainly a later addition. The term is used with reference to Jesus' relation to God in the Johannine writings of the New Testament. However, its inclusion here may represent more than a sudden desire to reflect Johannine usage. It may also function as a polemic against gnostics who, about the middle of the second century, distinguished between the celestial figure of God's only begotten Son and the historical figure of Jesus. The force of the expanded phrase, then, is to affirm that God's eternal and only Son is indeed to be identified with the earthly Jesus.

A similar interest also may be at work in the longer christological insertion following "our Lord":

> . . . who was conceived by the Holy Spirit, born of the Virgin Mary, suffered under Pontius Pilate, was crucified, dead and buried. On the third day he rose again from the dead, ascended into heaven. He sits at the right hand of God the Father Almighty, thence he will come to judge the living and the dead.

In a context of controversy, when some supported a Docetic view that the Son only appeared in human form but was not really human and did not really suffer, these words would be seen as a broad insistence on Christ's genuine humanity. Nevertheless, it should be recognized that most of this material goes back to the primitive kerygma of the apostolic age. So it may well be that the church at Rome saw the need to include this fuller christological statement in order that, on the occasion of their baptism, catechumens might summarize the fuller course of their instruction. Of course, these two lines of thinking need not be mutually exclusive; a controversial atmosphere might have contributed to other, less polemical motives for expansion.

In any case, at the beginning of the third century, the christological segment of the Roman creed affirms Christ Jesus as the only Son of the all-governing ruler of the universe, the virgin birth, the reality of Jesus' historical experiences, his lordship, his resurrection, and his role in the last judgment. It emphasizes the historic reality of Christ's sufferings and death, and this accords with a tendency in the west to view redemption as the overcoming of sin's death-grip on humanity through Christ's sacrifice. For our purposes, the key point is that this amalgam of biblical images and affirmations points toward the two general points of agreement that we noted earlier among New Testament writers. The Roman creed maintains the centrality of Jesus Christ by its insistence upon his exclusive divine sonship and virgin birth. There can be no question that Jesus Christ is decisive for God's converse with humanity. Likewise, by its insistence upon his suffering under Pontius Pilate, his crucifixion, resurrection, and ascension, the Roman creed maintains the particularity of Jesus Christ. There can be no question that divine sonship is to be ascribed to this particular historic figure who does and endures specific things.

No single eastern formula acquired a preeminent status similar to that of the Roman creed in the west, although there is sufficient family resemblance among the eastern creeds to speak of "an eastern type." An example is the formula offered by Eusebius of Caesarea in defense of his orthodoxy at the Council of Nicea. Something like it probably was in use at Caesarea from the second half of the third century:

> We believe in one God, the Father, Almighty, maker of all things visible and invisible; and in one lord Jesus Christ, the Logos of God, God from God, light from light, life from life, Son only begotten, first-begotten of all creation, begotten before all ages from the Father, through whom all things came into being, who because of our salvation was incarnate, and dwelt among men, and suffered, and rose again on the third day, and ascended to

the Father, and will rise again in glory to judge living and dead. We believe also in one Holy Spirit.[5]

In general, the creed used at Caesarea is more speculative and cosmic than the Roman. It emphasizes the oneness of God as the creator of all things visible and invisible. It underscores the precosmic begetting of the Son and the Son's participation in creation. It identifies the Logos or Son with Jesus Christ, "who was incarnate, and dwelt among men, and suffered, and rose again on the third day, and ascended to the Father." Interestingly, there is explicit mention of the incarnation in close association with "our salvation," and this accords with a tendency in the east to view redemption as a result of the incarnation itself.[6] Again, however, the key point I wish to make here is that an overall effect of the christological segment of the Caesarean formula is to intimate both the centrality and the particularity of Jesus Christ. There can be little doubt that our experience of the one who is "God from God," who was "begotten before all ages from the Father," and who "was incarnate, and dwelt among men" comprises a decisive and specific experience of God under the conditions of space and time. Indeed, the more speculative and cosmic tone of the eastern affirmation indicates the metaphysical lengths to which many in the east believed they were required to go in order to protect the centrality of Jesus Christ.

NICEA AND CHALCEDON: SPECIFYING CENTRALITY

Dramatic changes take place in the character and function of Christian creedal statements at the beginning of the fourth century. Now, the motive of combating heresy as well as imperial interests in maintaining peace among leaders of the established state religion come into prominence. The result is that the entire Roman world becomes the setting for doctrinal formulation.

Early in 312, the Emperor Constantine, who regarded his military victory over Maxentius for control of Rome as the result of Christ's power, granted Christians religious toleration and returned their confiscated churches and properties. Before the end of that year, he intervened in the Donatist controversy, unsuccessfully as it turned out, in an attempt to enforce ecclesiastical unity. When, in 324, Constantine's continued military successes made him sole ruler of the entire empire, he also had to contend with ecclesiastical controversy in the east. Receiving news of trouble in Alexandria between Bishop Alexander and the presbyter Arius, he sent a letter to the disputants. In it, the emperor apparently expressed his sorrow that "sharper controversies than those in Africa have arisen at Alexandria," although it appeared to him that they centered upon "questions of no importance and no use." Seeing that the human mind is "too weak to solve" these questions correctly, and that Alexander and Arius are substantially united on points of law and worship, he advised both men to forgive each other, noting that "philosophers of the same school had often differed in accessories."[7]

This tactic having failed, Constantine then proposed that the matter be settled by a council of bishops at Ancyra, but later changed the location to Nicea due to its greater accessibility. On 20 May 325, the first general council of the Christian church convened at the emperor's summons in Nicea.[8] According to Eusebius's *Life of Constantine,* the Christian emperor, whose military victories had recently reunited the Roman Empire, stood before the fathers at the opening session. Appearing "as a messenger from God, covered in gold and precious stones," he outlined the agenda "in a gentle voice." The emperor spoke in Latin and, at his side, an assistant translated into Greek. He noted that it was his "greatest pleasure" to see the bishops assembled, that he considered "disunion in the Church an evil more terrible and more grievous than any kind of war," and that, upon being told of the division that had arisen, he had resolved to attend to this matter before all else. He concluded with an exhortation:

> Do not hesitate, my friends—do not hesitate, ye servants of God; banish all causes of dissention—solve controversial difficulties according to the law of peace, so as to accomplish the work which shall be most agreeable to God, and cause me, your fellow-servant, infinite joy.[9]

With the Council of Nicea precedent was set for the practice of clerics gathering together in assemblies representing the church at large to author statements of agreement on matters of doctrine and ecclesiastical law, as well as for the involvement of the emperor in such assemblies. The acts of these councils had more than local authority

and could be enforced by the state. Nevertheless, it was not the intention of the fathers at Nicea to supersede the local confessions. "As
C. H. Turner put it, 'The old creeds were for catechumens, the new
creed was a creed for bishops.' It was devised as the touchstone by
which the doctrines of Church teachers and leaders might be certified
as correct."[10]

The decisions of Nicea reveal a church engaged in the wide-
ranging business of ordering both its life and its dogma. The council
accepted the date for Easter in use at Rome and Alexandria.[11] Among
its twenty canons were some concerning appointments to ecclesiastical
offices, for example, that priests and bishops not be chosen from
among those who have "just turned from a heathen life to the faith"
(2), and that bishops be appointed by all other bishops in a province
and, in the case that all cannot meet together for this purpose, at least
three do so with the written consent of the rest (4). The twentieth
canon attempted to standardize worship, with such decrees as "all shall
offer prayers standing" in services from Easter to Pentecost. Still others
concerned matters of conduct, for example, that clerics accept no interest on money "no matter on what grounds" (17), that they share
their houses only with women who "are free from all suspicion," such
as their natural mothers and sisters (3), and that those who castrate
themselves be required to resign their posts (1).[12]

With respect to the trouble at Alexandria, the council came down
squarely against Arius, whom it banished, although this hardly put
an end to his influence. Doctrinally, the fathers affirmed, *contra* Arius
and his supporters who subordinated the Son to the Father in the name
of strict monotheism, that the "one Lord Jesus Christ, the Son of
God" is "from the essence of the Father, God from God, Light from
Light, true God from true God." He is the one "who for us men and
for our salvation came down and was incarnate, becoming human."
In case this left any doubt about the heretical particulars of Arian
teaching, the fathers added the following:

> But, those who say, once he was not, or he was not before his
> generation, or he came to be out of nothing, or who assert that
> he, the Son of God, is of a different *hypostasis* or *ousia,* or that he
> is a creature, or changeable or mutable, the Catholic and Apostolic
> Church anathematizes them.[13]

Essentially, the council took up a local baptismal creed of the eastern type and inserted into it clauses directed against the Arians.[14] The key anti-Arian clause affirmed that Jesus Christ, the Son of God, is "of the same essence as the Father" (*homoousion to patri*). Interestingly, it was precisely with the critical word *homoousios* that the council introduced a novel term with which even many of the non-Arians were uncomfortable. Athanasius (d. 373) later recollected that the fathers would have preferred to express themselves in biblical language but that, whatever scriptural phrases were proposed, the Arians managed to interpret them their own way.[15]

Thus, the first council to define orthodoxy in the sense of a general standard for Christian teaching found it necessary to adopt a progressive theology, precisely in order to express what it took to be an essential affirmation of biblical faith. Evidently, in the intellectual and cultural climate of the Hellenistic world, continuity with the apostolic tradition was deemed to require doctrinal innovation. A mere repetition of the language of the received tradition actually would have served the cause of heresy. Nicea's opponents were well aware of this. Indeed, in 357, when Arianism was again on the rise and the Nicene Creed itself subjected to open criticism, the Third Synod of Sirmium banned the use of *homoousios* in Christian preaching for the reason that it is not contained in scripture.[16]

For our purposes, the chief significance of *homoousios* is that it represents a further specification of the centrality of Jesus Christ. Arius and his supporters preferred the phrase "of *like* essence with the Father" (*homoiousion to patri*). This would have protected strict monotheism from trinitarian complexities, but it also would have loosened the sense in which Jesus Christ is decisive for God's converse with humanity. By contrast, the fathers at Nicea chose a metaphysical expression of Christ's divinity that leaves no doubt about his decisiveness for our apprehension of God. Here, in this individual, under the conditions of space and time, God's very reality (and not just something like it) has been made available to us.

By the time of the Council at Chalcedon in 451, the Nicene Creed had acquired the standing of a basic statement of the incarnation, but now the cutting edge of theological debate concerned more subtle questions. Essentially, two ways of conceiving the constitution of the incarnate Christ had come to the fore.[17] One, which was in favor at Alexandria, envisioned a vital conjunction of Logos and flesh. Here "flesh" was sometimes taken to signify a human body without a soul. Thus, for Apollinarius (d. ca. 390), the Logos dwelt in the flesh, taking the place of the human soul or *nous* and governing the flesh that bears it; the heavenly and earthly elements are therefore parts of a single whole. Indeed, Apollinarius refers to Christ's "one nature" *(mia physis)*. From the later perspective of Chalcedon, the strength of this line of thinking is that it clearly upholds the unity of the incarnate Christ. Its weaknesses are that it compromises the fullness of Christ's humanity (can his humanity be complete if he has no rational soul?), and also may imply that, in the incarnation, divinity and humanity are transformed into a third reality. The other way of thinking, in favor at Antioch and of which Nestorius (d. after 451) was a representative, envisioned the incarnation as a conjunction of Logos and man. Here, the human element is thought to have a soul and is therefore a complete man, rather than mere flesh. Thus, Nestorius sees Christ as the sum of two complete natures whose diverse characteristics are joined in one *prosopon* or countenance. From the later perspective of Chalcedon, the strength of this line of thinking is that it protects the fullness of the two natures. Its difficulty is that the weak understanding of *prosopon* makes for an ambiguous account of Christ's oneness or unity.[18]

Before Chalcedon took place, the Alexandrian approach was significantly amended and refined. Athanasius did not deny the soul of Christ, but simply said that "[the Word] became man and did not come into a man."[19] Cyril of Alexandria (d. 444) positively affirmed the soul of Christ.[20] Indeed, when defending himself against the charge of Apollinarianism, he also was willing to admit the validity of talk about two natures "united without separation, without confusion, and without transformation."[21]

From the later perspective of Chalcedon, it is notable that neither Cyril nor his Antiochene opponents were able to distinguish between two fundamental terms. Both *physis* and "hypostasis" carried connotations of "nature" and "substance." The Antiochenes reserved these words to refer to the duality of Christ's natures, and spoke of unity only at the level of Christ's *prosopon,* his outward aspect or form. In the absence of any clear statement regarding an ontological basis for this unity, however, it appeared to the Alexandrians that the Antiochenes were implying two ontological subjects in Christ's one countenance or appearance. This the Alexandrians regarded as soteriologically disastrous because, for them, redemption was understood as the elevation of human nature by its ontological union with the divine in the incarnation itself. On the other hand, although Cyril sometimes distinguished between the two natures in the incarnate Christ, in order to express a strong ontological unity (and also because he mistakenly attributed the phrase to Athanasius), he continued to speak also of "one nature incarnate of God the Word." To the Antiochenes, this expression implied that Christ was not really human at all.

At this point, Latin theology made its signal contribution partly because it operated with a different vocabulary in a different tongue. In his *Tome to Flavian,* Leo of Rome (d. 461) insisted that Christ was one *persona* or indivisible Son of God, who exists in two natures, at the same time God and man. The fathers at Chalcedon aligned Leo's unified *persona* with "hypostasis," while they also acknowledged one Lord Jesus Christ "in two natures" *(en duo physesin).* An ontological unity of Christ, so essential to the Alexandrian tradition, was therefore maintained at the level of the person *(prosopon),* even as a distinction at the level of natures *(physesin),* so dear to the Antiochenes, was also affirmed.

Therefore, the formal confession of faith approved at Chalcedon was truly ecumenical in the sense that all of the major trends of contemporary theology contributed to it.[22] Here is the celebrated statement:

> Following, then, the holy Fathers, we all with one voice teach that it should be confessed that our Lord Jesus Christ is one and the same Son, the Same perfect in Godhead, the Same perfect in manhood, truly God and truly man, the Same [consisting] of a rational soul and a body; *homoousios* with the Father as to his Godhead, and the Same *homoousios* with us as to his manhood; in all things like unto us, sin only excepted; begotten of the Father before all ages as to his Godhead, and in the last days, the Same, for us and for our salvation, of Mary the Virgin *Theotokos* [God-bearer] as to his manhood;

> One and the same Christ, Son, Lord, Only-begotten, made
> known in two natures [which exist] without confusion, without
> change, without division, without separation; the difference of
> the natures having been in no wise taken away by reason of the
> union, but rather the properties of each being preserved, and
> [both] concurring into one Person *(prosopon)* and one *hypostasis*—
> not parted or divided into two Persons *(prosopoa),* but one and
> the same Son and Only-begotten, the divine Logos, the Lord Jesus
> Christ; even as the prophets from of old [have spoken] concerning
> him, and as the Lord Jesus Christ himself has taught us, and as
> the Symbol of the Fathers has delivered to us.[23]

With this compromise solution, orthodoxy took yet another startlingly innovative turn, one that demanded a reconsideration of the basic
meanings of christological discourse's fundamental terms. Essentially,
with the benefit of recourse to western theology, the fathers drew a
"new and revolutionary" distinction between *physis* and "hypostasis."
Yet the precise significance of this distinction was far from settled.[24]
Indeed, one commentator concludes that the fathers' grasp of their
formula was intuitive. "None of them could have given a definition
of the concepts with which they now expressed christological dogma"
and they made "no attempt at a philosophical definition or speculative
analysis!"[25]

As with the deliberations at Nicea, a summary of the main doctrinal issues at Chalcedon tells only a part of the story. Controversy
took a serious turn when, in November 448, an influential monk
named Eutyches was summoned to appear before the First Synod of
Constantinople, which had been convened by the Bishop Flavian of
that city, himself a supporter of the Antiochene position.[26] Eutyches'
actual doctrine is difficult to determine, though it is clear that his
thought was generally of the Alexandrian type.[27] Apparently, the aged
monk held that the union of the incarnation was "from two natures,"
but that, after the union, there was only one nature.[28] Indeed, he is
reputed to have asked the synod's messengers where in scripture the
expression "two natures" is to be found, and to have insisted that he
would suffer anything rather than confess it.[29] When, after having
declined a number of summonses, the accused hermit finally did appear
before the synod, he was deposed from his office even as he appealed
to writings of Athanasius and Cyril in his own defense, and the doctrine that there is but one nature after the union was condemned.[30]

Eutyches may have been old but he was not politically naive. He quickly appealed to the bishops of Rome, Alexandria, Jerusalem, and Thessalonica. At Rome, Leo responded by favoring Flavian and writing his famous *Tome,* which sets out his own understanding of the incarnation in opposition to Eutyches. At Alexandria, however, Bishop Dioscorus sided with Eutyches, flatly refused to acknowledge the judgment of the Constantinopolitan synod, and induced Theodosius the Younger, emperor in the east, to summon a general council to take place at Ephesus in August 449. The emperor appointed Dioscorus president of the council, even though the meeting was to take place in the local jurisdiction of Flavian.[31]

The proceedings of the Council at Ephesus—Leo called it the "Robber Synod"—were tumultuous, and its irregularities were later censured by the fathers at Chalcedon. Many of those who held the two-natures doctrine and had been influential at Constantinople less than a year earlier were either barred from the council altogether or forbidden to vote. Leo, who did not attend, sent legates with a copy of his *Tome,* but Dioscorus, who apparently ruled the proceedings with a heavy hand, kept it from being read.[32] Eutyches was vindicated. The two-natures confession was anathematized, and its leading advocates, including Flavian, who subsequently died, were condemned and deposed.

In October 449, Leo wrote to the Emperor Theodosius asking that another general council be held in Italy, and that, until then, everything remain as it was before the recent meeting at Ephesus. Theodosius refused, and he stated further that Flavian and the others had been justly deposed, and that peace would be maintained in the church only if the decisions of Ephesus were upheld.[33] Suddenly, however, on 28 July 450, Theodosius died as the result of a fall from his horse. He had no son, and so was succeeded by his sister, Pulcheria, who agreed to take a resolute and distinguished military officer, Marcian, as her consort and co-regent. The new emperor believed that the power accorded the Alexandrian see under Theodosius's reign would make difficulties for his own administration, and took actions aimed at making the capital city of Constantinople supreme in the east. By the end of the year, Flavian's body was returned to Constantinople and buried with great honor in the Basilica of the Apostles, and an imperial order was given that those deposed at Ephesus were to be reinstated following a meeting of another general council. The clergy at Constantinople were induced to accept Leo's *Tome,* and many eastern bishops reconsidered the wisdom of their actions under Dioscorus's leadership at Ephesus.[34]

Marcian summoned a general council to be held at Nicea on 1 September 451. His edict stated that "the true faith and orthodox religion is to be preferred to everything else. For if God is gracious to us, then our Empire will be firmly established." It also made explicit, favorable mention of Leo's letters.[35] Commencement of the council was delayed because the emperor was occupied with other matters, and its location was changed to Chalcedon because that town was near enough to the capital to allow Marcian to attend in person "both to the business in Constantinople and to that of the Council."[36] When the council did open on 8 October 451, eighteen imperial commissioners were present.[37] During the first session, it was decided that Flavian and the others had been unjustly condemned at Ephesus. It was decided too, subject to the emperor's approval, that Dioscorus and his ardent supporters should be deposed. Also, and most significantly, the imperial commissioners insisted that a discussion of the true faith take place at the next meeting and listed the writings that the emperor considered orthodox. Two days later, the majority of the fathers present favored a simple reaffirmation of Nicea, and they protested the suggestion that they should write a new formulary of the faith. The imperial commissioners, however, were unmoved, and documents including the Creed of Nicea, letters by Cyril, and Leo's *Tome* were read and approved.[38] At the third session, those friendly to Dioscorus were absent. Many accusations were brought against the Alexandrian patriarch and he was deposed "from his episcopal office, and deprived of all spiritual functions."[39]

Meanwhile, at the direction of the imperial commissioners, a group had been working for some time on a doctrinal statement aimed at settling disputed questions. That group reached agreement on 21 October, and their statement was presented at the council's fifth session on the following day. Apparently, however, the papal legates had no hand in its final composition, and the document took a decidedly Cyrillian, anti-Nestorian stance. The majority of the fathers favored the document, but Leo's legates strenuously objected, threatening to leave the council altogether and hold a local synod at Rome. Much discussion followed. The imperial commissioners, anxious to conciliate the west, consulted with the emperor. They then appointed another committee to revise the statement. This group met for a period of time unspecified in the minutes and returned on the same day with the final text of the Chalcedonian Definition that was accepted by all.[40]

Both the Emperor Marcian and the Empress Pulcheria were present at the sixth session on 25 October. In a short statement, Marcian said he had summoned the present council "that all error and all obscurity might be dispelled," and that in the future no one should teach anything else concerning the incarnation than what was contained in the Creed of Nicea and testified to in Leo's *Tome* to Flavian. He had followed, he said, the example of Constantine in being present at the council for the purpose of strengthening the faith. The fathers exclaimed their approval. The emperor then asked whether the formula presented the view of all. The bishops answered that it did and added, "Prosperity to Marcian, the new Constantine, the new Paul, the new David!" Stopping just short of an even more impressive title, they also said, "You are the peace of the world!" The emperor then gave thanks to Christ that unity had been restored, "and threatened all, as well private men and soldiers as the clergy, with heavy punishment if they should again stir up controversies respecting the faith." He also proposed three laws. The first forbade clerics from occupying themselves in worldly business for the sake of gain. The second required that monasteries be founded only with the consent of the local bishop. The third required that, but for exceptional circumstances, clerics remain attached to the local church they were first authorized to serve. These were taken up by the council into its third, fourth, and twentieth canons. In all, before its final session on 1 November, the council approved thirty canons regulating practical matters.[41]

This brief review of the circumstances surrounding Chalcedon shows that its celebrated definition is a fruit of compromise in which theology and politics are inextricably intertwined. The main parties to the compromise were four: the Alexandrians, the Antiochenes, the western bishops led by Leo of Rome, and the Emperor Marcian himself, whose interests were ably represented by his imperial commissioners. True, the language of the definition reflects compromise among the great theological centers of the church; but that it was written at all is testimony to the force of the emperor's conviction that ecclesiastical unity could be established by the general acceptance of a specific doctrinal formula.[42] Moreover, that the final draft was not simply another Cyrillian statement directed against the Antiochenes, but one that accommodated Leo's insistence upon the two natures and so left room for an Antiochene contribution, was due largely to the emperor's understanding of the imperial interest.

Thus, an appreciation for the imperial interest in the doctrinal unity of the church contributes to our understanding of the historic limits at Chalcedon that demanded restraint. On the one side, the fathers were constrained by the limits of political compromise. Any detailed account of the incarnation in Alexandrian, Antiochene, or Roman terms would have seriously offended one or another camp. By itself, this fact was not determinative since, as we may surmise from the near acceptance of the first draft at the council's critical fifth session, the majority of the fathers in attendance, even after Dioscorus's departure, were Alexandrian in their thinking. When coupled with the emperor's insistence upon a formula agreeable to all, however, it meant that no detailed account of the incarnation was politically possible. On the other side, the fathers were restrained by the intellectual limits of their own understanding of the terminology they now had introduced into the compromise formula. Many in attendance could have given a fuller account of the incarnation in Alexandrian, Antiochene, or Roman terms, but few if any had sufficient grasp of the new vocabulary to give a detailed account in Chalcedonian terms. Operating within these political and intellectual limits, then, the Chalcedonian fathers did not frame a full theology of the incarnation so much as a compromise formula that might guide further statements. Indeed, it is difficult to see how they could have done otherwise in the absence of clear philosophical definitions of key terms such as *physis,* "hypostasis," and *prosopon.*[43]

Theologically, the definition hardly settles all speculative questions about the relationship between the divinity and humanity of the incarnate Christ; nor does it dispel the mystery of the incarnation. Instead, it furnishes a basic framework that gives direction to further attempts to speak about Jesus Christ.[44] There is a strong affirmation of Christ's divinity, as there had also been at Nicea, only now this is combined with an exactly parallel affirmation of Christ's humanity and a more complex insistence upon the unity of Christ's person. For the fathers at Chalcedon, Jesus Christ is "*homoousios* with the Father as to his Godhead, and . . . *homoousios* with us as to his manhood." Jesus Christ is truly God and truly man, two natures united in one hypostasis. There can be no question, then, that he is central and decisive not only for our apprehension of God but also for our apprehension of what it is to be human in appropriate relation to God.

The historical development leading up to this signal affirmation proved startlingly innovative in its introduction of new terms and concepts into christological dogma, routinely practical in its attention to ordering the life of the church, and eminently political in terms both of ecclesiastical and imperial issues. Again, the resultant doctrine was not entirely speculative, if by "speculation" one means abstract conjecture as opposed to practical knowledge. The two-natures formula told Christians to look to this one person, Jesus Christ, for their fundamental visions of God and humanity. Here, they apprehended the ultimate reality with which every person must deal, and here they also saw how human beings might be truly responsive to that reality. Moreover, the constitution of Christ's person was perceived to be of crucial importance for salvation. Human nature, threatened as it is by temporal ambiguities, was thought to be elevated by its union with the eternal divine nature. Redemption, or the assumption of human nature into incorruption by its union with the divine, was construed as an ontological process established in the incarnation itself, and therefore metaphysical reflections about the constitution of the incarnate Christ became a vital matter of practical significance. This, finally, was the existential issue of piety behind the Alexandrians' attachment to the *mia physis* formula, and it is preserved in the Chalcedonian Definition by the insistence upon one hypostasis.

Chalcedon's delicate balance required both defense and further development during the following centuries. The unity of Christ was underscored by varied appeals to "the communication of properties," which affirmed that each nature imparted its characteristic properties to the person of the incarnate Logos. Nevertheless, the redeemer's genuine humanity seemed compromised by periodic assertions of monotheletism, or the view that the divine will alone energized the person of Christ. Maximus of Rome and others responded by asserting dyotheletism, or the view that, in assuming human nature, the Logos also assumed a human will.[45] Some depictions of Christ's genuine humanity also came in for censure. For example, the Spanish adoptionists Elipandus and Felix maintained that, unlike his divinity, Christ's flesh was created and subsequently adopted rather than begotten from the essence of the Father. Although their motive was to avoid any hint of Docetism, others feared the implications of the "Spanish error" for the unity of Christ. Orthodox theologians therefore responded by claiming that Christ's human nature was one person with the Father from its inception, and that the flesh assumed by God is the nature of a man but unlike other ordinary men.[46] The result was an understanding of Christ's humanity that protected his perfection by claiming that, because of his virgin birth, Christ was the only one who had not been mired in Adam's fall.

Anselm of Canterbury, in a move that foreshadowed the later Protestant emphasis on Christ's work, pressed the two-natures doctrine into the service of the atonement by insisting upon the indispensable contributions of each nature to the work of redemption.[47] Throughout the medieval period, a strand of piety represented by Thomas à Kempis and others emphasized following Christ's example in this life, although the persistent tendency was to despise the body and to transfer affections toward invisible, spiritual realities.[48] The later medieval scholastics worked to systematize the orthodox teachings about Christ's person that were handed down to them.

PROTESTANT REFORMERS:
THEMATIZING PARTICULARITY

Both Martin Luther and John Calvin proved strong supporters of Chalcedon, although one discerns in their writings a certain discomfort with what they perceive to be the rather speculative and abstract tone of the classical formulas. Luther, whose theology of the cross underscored Christ's "conquest of sin, death and the devil," could wax polemical about medieval attempts to get ever more precise about the relation between Christ's two natures:

> What difference does that make to me? That he is man and God
> by nature, that he has for his own self; but that he has exercised
> his office and poured out his love, becoming my Savior and
> Redeemer—that happens for my consolation and benefit.[49]

Similarly, Calvin finds terms such as *homoousios* and *prosopon* "necessary to unmask false teachers," though he "could wish they were
buried if only" people would agree about essentials of the faith.[50] Some
of the more creative christological sections of Calvin's *Institutes* discuss
the functions of Christ as the mediator who restores "us to God's grace
as to make of the children of men, children of God," and Calvin insists
that a right understanding of Christ's activity is "a firm basis for
salvation."[51]

The tendency toward discomfort with what they perceive to be
the abstract tone of the conciliar formulas is partly a result of the
reformers' break with medieval scholasticism:

> Disillusionment with the inherited scholastic style was one respect
> in which Erasmus, Luther, and Calvin were all at one, despite
> their difference: they agreed that the logic chopping and idle
> speculation of the "sophists" had to yield to study of the earliest
> Christian documents, the springs of genuine piety.[52]

The Reformation emphasis on scripture once again made people pain-
fully aware that some of the central terms and concepts of the inherited
christological dogma were not entirely biblical. Renewed attention to
the Bible also focused greater attention on Paul's understanding of
redemption in Christ and on the narrative portraits of Jesus in the
Gospels. In this context, terms such as *physis* and "hypostasis" were
bound to look a bit heady and abstract.

Even more fundamentally, perhaps, that terms and concepts that
once had cut to the very heart of Christian believing were now regarded
with even the slightest tinge of suspicion reflects the fact that sixteenth-
century Protestantism subtly recast piety's leading concerns. For Luther, the question of redemption was raised most poignantly not by
a perceived contrast between temporality and eternity but by the experience of a tortured conscience unrelieved by the righteousness of
his own works.[53] Luther's most basic estimate of Christ's significance
comes through in his famous hymn, "Did we in our own strength
confide, our striving would be losing." The center of attention shifts

from the ontology of Christ's person toward a more activist apprehension of Christ's role in winning the decisive victory over sin and
vouchsafing the free justification of sinners. And, while there are
important differences between Luther and Calvin, the Genevan re-
former shared Luther's theology of grace even as he turned it toward
the task of ordering the Christian life with careful attention to sanc-
tification and social structures. For Calvin, "the purpose of theology
is to edify, to transform human life and society."[54] When he speaks of
the ontology of Christ's person, more often than not his aim is to
show how the two natures are necessary if Christ is to function as the
mediator who, by his sacrificial obedience, reconciles God and man.[55]

In general, "it seems fair to say that Reformation theology . . .
subordinates the incarnation to the atonement," and therefore stresses
the historical particularity of what Jesus Christ does and endures. "The
accent is not on a process of divinization begun in the incarnation but
on the removal of the penalty of sin by the death of Christ."[56] The
resultant emphasis upon Christ's work of reconciliation is representative of the shift that takes place in piety's chief concerns, and it goes
hand in hand with what we have called the particularity of Jesus Christ.
If the Chalcedonian Definition insists that Jesus Christ is central for
our apprehensions of God and of human life in appropriate relation
to God, then Reformation christology seems especially concerned that
these apprehensions be referred specifically to the life, ministry, death,
and resurrection of Jesus Christ.

There was precedent for this emphasis. The Roman creed stressed
the earthly reality of Jesus' life, sufferings, and death, even to the
extent of insisting upon a historic point in time for his crucifixion
"under Pontius Pilate." At least since the time of Augustine, emphasis
in the west had fallen on Christ's function as the mediator who suffers
and is sacrificed for our sins that we might be reconciled to God.[57]
So, for example, Anselm's classic argument, that the God-man is
necessary because no one can make the needed satisfaction for sin
except God and no one ought to make it except man, is an attempt
to demonstrate the intelligibility of the two-natures doctrine from a
prior conviction about Christ's work of atonement.[58]

Attention to the particulars of what Jesus Christ says, does, and
endures calls for doctrinal summarization, and this often has been done

with the aid of the symbols of king and priest, or prophet, king, and priest. A twofold pattern predominates for a number of writers, including Augustine, Luther, and Philip Melanchthon. Although different writers introduce varied subtleties, essentially Christ as king is thought to establish a new law and to govern the Christian life, while as priest he is the one who, by his ministry of a new holiness and his intercession, makes this life possible by rendering sinners acceptable in God's sight. Thus, for example, Augustine says that "He is king because he rules and leads us; he is priest because he makes intercession for us."[59]

Threefold patterns appear in Thomas Aquinas's *Summa Theologiae* and in the 1559 edition of Calvin's *Institutes of the Christian Religion*. They are foreshadowed in a number of patristic writers, including John Chrysostum and Justin Martyr, and have subsequently been used by Reformed, Lutheran, Anglican, and Roman Catholic thinkers, including the authors of the Heidelberg Catechism and the Westminster Confession, as well as Bishop Butler, Friedrich Schleiermacher, Cardinal Newman, and Emil Brunner. Threefold patterns also are present among some of Calvin's contemporaries, including Viret, Osiander, and Bucer.[60]

Again, different writers develop threefold patterns in a variety of ways. Aquinas calls Christ lawgiver, priest, and king, though he gives priority to the priestly function. As mediator, says Aquinas, Christ unites people with God by "setting before man the divine commandments and gifts and by atoning and interceding for men with God."[61] Calvin calls Christ prophet, king, and priest. As prophet, Christ is the "herald and witness of the Father's grace," the teacher who brings a perfect wisdom that puts an end to all prophecy. As king, Christ rules the Christian life "inwardly and outwardly," shares with us what he has received, and clothes us with his righteousness. As priest, he is "a pure and stainless mediator . . . an everlasting intercessor who, by his death, reconciles us to God."[62]

Perhaps the most important difference between the twofold and threefold patterns is that the latter, under the title of prophet, draws attention more directly to Christ as teacher and example.[63] Still, it would be easy to make too much of this. There is no unanimity on where to locate Christ's teaching activity among those who employ

threefold patterns. Aquinas tends to subsume teaching under the priestly image. Calvin never does much with his threefold pattern once it
is introduced into his *Institutes,* and a twofold schematization of priest
and king predominates in his commentaries. Nevertheless, whether
he presents his reflections about Christ's work in twofold or threefold
form, Calvin consistently regards Jesus as teacher and master.[64] Similarly, it would be unfair to many of those who present a twofold
pattern to suggest that they neglect Christ's teaching and example.
Augustine emphasizes the exemplary aspect of Christ's work as one
who embodies the humility of God and shows sinners how far they
have departed from the truth. He also regards Christ as the teacher
who, in his Sermon on the Mount, communicates "the perfect standard
of the Christian life."[65] Martin Luther writes that "Scripture presents
Christ in two ways: first, as a gift . . . ; secondly, as an example for
us to imitate."[66]

For our purposes, the critical point is that both the twofold and
threefold patterns are theological constructs that orchestrate or guide
faithful reflection about the particularity of Jesus Christ. Their function
is symbolically to express the patterned unity of what Jesus Christ
says, does, and endures, and so to insist that our decisive apprehensions
of God and of human life in responsive relation to God be referred to
the specific features and characteristics of the Jesus Christ who is
presented in the New Testament. The prominence of twofold and
threefold schematizations of Christ's work, especially among representatives of Protestant Christianity, is indicative of a shift in piety's
chief concern away from incarnation and deification and toward reconciliation and Christ's function in bringing about redemption from
the power of sin and in reorienting human life around a true devotional
center.

LIBERALS AND CONTEMPORARIES:
FUNDAMENTAL CRITICISMS

The shift away from incarnation and deification forms an essential
part of the background for the christological bent of liberal Protestantism. Schleiermacher, Albrecht Ritschl, Adolf Harnack, Walter
Rauschenbusch, and others tended to see in the Reformation at least

the beginning of a turn away from abstract speculation toward experience and practice. Thus, Schleiermacher commended Calvin's *Institutes* because it never loses sight of the religious affections, Ritschl regarded the believer's continual experience of forgiveness as the center of Luther's theology, and Rauschenbusch believed the doctrine of vocation to be a decisive contribution that turned Christians toward service in the world.[67] The visions of the Reformation put forward by each of these men responded to certain signal features of their own situation. The turn toward experience was sharpened by the antimetaphysical bias in modern philosophy following the works of David Hume and Immanuel Kant, as well as by a new appreciation for the dynamics and particularities of history that was abetted by the emergence of critical-historical and social scholarship.[68] The commitment to theology as a practical enterprise whose purpose it is to transform human life and society was intensified by continuing pressures under the impact of industrialization to address a variety of circumstances that came to be known as the "social problem" or "social question."

All in all, few things could have been less amenable to the ethos of the age than the concern for a disjunction between temporality and eternity that had animated Hellenistic piety in its deliberations about Christ's natures. Instead, history itself now became the realm in which meaning was sought, and attention in christology was focused ever more sharply upon reconciliation and regeneration. Jesus Christ was looked upon as the one who enables people to take up a true and godly form of life in the world. The emphasis fell not on the metaphysical constitution of Christ's person but upon the power of his personality to bring people into communion with God and one another. What had appeared to the reformers as an abstract tinge now seemed unworkably speculative. Whether the metaphysically suffused two-natures doctrine had any retrievable meaning at all seemed questionable. With the rise of historical scholarship, the subject of christology was perceived to be the historical figure of Jesus to whom the Gospels attest. And, when the liberals investigated the Gospels, the Jesus they found seemed at odds with the Christ of the Chalcedonian Definition. No single writer can speak to this point for the liberal movement as a whole, but the following statement by Rauschenbusch captures something of its spirit:

> The social gospel is not primarily interested in metaphysical questions; its christological interest is all for a real personality who could set a great historical process in motion; it wants his work interpreted by the purposes which ruled and directed his active life; it would have more interest in basing the divine quality of his personality on free and ethical acts of his will than in dwelling on the passive inheritance of a divine essence.[69]

For the liberal theologians of the nineteenth and twentieth centuries, a historical regard for the particularity of Jesus Christ took priority over metaphysical articulations of his centrality. Indeed, the particular things that Jesus of Nazareth said, did, and endured were thought to furnish a more reliable and more biblical basis for the affirmation that Jesus Christ is central and decisive than could possibly be provided by an abstract ontology of his person. During the twentieth century, it is true, the liberals' easy confidence that the New Testament affords adequate access to the Jesus of history would be sharply challenged. Yet this did not mean that the way was cleared for a naive return to the metaphysical terms of Hellenistic dogma. Accordingly, from the nineteenth century to the present day, the classical formulas have been subjected to a spate of related criticisms and emendations.

A first objection is that Chalcedon's metaphysical language is too far removed from the dynamics of history and the experience of faith. Therefore, Schleiermacher treats the traditional formulas as "products of controversy" that often fail to maintain a close relation to the interests of Christian piety.[70] Harnack, who regards Hellenistic speculation as an intrusion upon the Gospel, maintains that "the victory of the Nicene Creed was a victory of the priests over the faith of the Christian people," and that "Christ as *homoousios* became a dogmatic form of words" that was out of touch with lived Christianity.[71]

Those who continue to affirm the importance of metaphysical language in theology nevertheless criticize the particular terms of the traditional formulas, because these terms are informed by the static category of substance. Thus, Paul Tillich, who employs a dynamic ontology in the service of Christian theology, finds the specific meta-physical conceptuality of the orthodox statements outmoded, as do many contemporaries whose work is informed by the process phi-losophies of Alfred North Whitehead and Charles Hartshorne.[72] Al-though he can hardly be called a philosophical thinker in the same sense as either Tillich or the process theologians, Karl Barth's under-standing of God's being and activity also represents a move toward a more dynamic and historical conception of God and a break with more traditional and static conceptions. A similar point might also be made about the implications for christology of Emil Brunner's understanding of God as the supreme subject who communicates God's self in acts of self-disclosure. For both Barth and Brunner, Jesus Christ is God's decisive act in history, and neither theologian claims that an impassible divine nature was united with a passible human nature.[73] Reinhold Niebuhr dispenses with what he calls "the impossibility" of rendering metaphysically plausible the doctrine that Jesus was both human and divine. This impossibility, says Niebuhr,

> is fully attested by the ages of Christological controversy in which Christian thought sought futilely to express the idea that Christ was fully human and yet transcended the human. This controversy produced a long series of heresies. . . . The heresies were refuted by orthodox affirmations which were forced to commit them-selves to metaphysical absurdities.[74]

In sum, many have come to believe that the terminology of the tra-ditional formulas represents the thought form of a particular time and place, which is finally inadequate for reflection about the historic reality of Jesus Christ.

A second objection is that the traditional formulas are not com-patible with the humanity of Jesus portrayed in the Gospels. A number of modern theologians point out that, particularly under the influence of early Alexandrian formulas, some patristic thinkers speak of the generic or nonpersonal humanity of the incarnate Christ. Although Jesus is human, he is not, strictly speaking, a man, since the divine Word forms the center of his person and the "flesh" does not. Others are troubled by what it means to say, following the monothelite con-troversy, that there are two wills in Jesus Christ. Still others wonder about implications of the assertion, following Spanish adoptionism, that the human nature of the incarnate Christ is fundamentally different from that of all other people. Moreover, it is common to find in the classical tradition affirmations of Christ's omniscience as well as interpretations of his perfection that appear to deny the reality of his inner conflicts with disobedience and sin. In the Synoptic Gospels, however, Jesus is portrayed as a truly human person who confesses limitations of his knowledge (Mark 13:32), overcomes genuine temptations to sin, and is troubled about God's will for him at Gethsemane.

Harnack has difficulties such as these in mind when he says that the Hellenistic christology "has scarcely any connexion with the Jesus Christ of the Gospel, and its formulas do not fit him." [75] Schleiermacher tries to uphold the humanness of Jesus' intellectual, moral, and religious life by affirming that Jesus was, in all respects, subject to principles of organic growth. [76] Barth claims that even the early patristic formulas never meant that the incarnate Christ had no personality in the modern sense, and he departs from a segment of orthodox tradition when he claims that the Word assumed fallen human nature (flesh) in the incarnation. [77] Reinhold Niebuhr says flatly that "it is not possible to assert the sinlessness of every individual act of any historical character," and he subjects the affirmation of Christ's sinless perfection to extensive criticism and reinterpretation. [78]

In sum, many believe that the traditional formulas, despite their intentions to the contrary, tend toward a subtle Docetism that is not compatible with Jesus' genuine humanity and is out of kilter with many New Testament accounts. Recently the issue has been raised again by Maurice Wiles in his contributions to *The Myth of God Incarnate*. Wiles contends that the traditional picture of Jesus Christ cannot be regarded as "recognizably human." [79]

Finally, there are those who complain that the orthodox formulas impede a satisfactory explanation of the relation between Jesus' humanity and divinity. Here again we should note that the Chalcedonian Definition itself does not address the question of how the two natures operated during the incarnation. Nevertheless, the doctrine articulated at Chalcedon has consistently made for difficulties among those who have tried to address that question. This is one of the reasons why John Hick argues that the orthodox tradition has been unable to specify the semantic content of its talk about Jesus as God and man. Somewhat as Harnack regards the doctrine of Christ as *homoousios,* Hick finds the two-natures doctrine to be "a form of words without assignable meaning."[80]

Even if one agrees with Schubert Ogden that Hick's judgment is "perhaps extreme," one nevertheless may admit that there are significant difficulties with the way that the two-natures formula has functioned in Christian tradition.[81] Leo's understanding of the reciprocal operation of the two natures does not allow both to be expressed in everything Jesus did and endured. Indeed, nothing Jesus did or endured is more crucial for the work of redemption than his suffering and death on the cross, yet precisely here the unity of the two natures becomes especially suspect, since Leo can only say that the one nature is capable of death while the other is not. Exactly what Cyril's statements about the impassible suffering of the Logos may mean for the participation of divinity in Jesus' sufferings is rather confusing. Many would agree with the judgment of G. W. H. Lampe that

> the weakness of the Christological tradition of Athanasius, and Alexandria generally, becomes apparent again in Cyril at this point; the presuppositions, that the subject of the Gospel record is the Logos and that deity is impassible, can be reconciled only by ascribing suffering exclusively to the flesh. Hence Cyril's treatment of Gethsemane and the Temptations is inadequate.[82]

Although it was certainly not the intention of the fathers at Chalcedon to render the unity of Christ's person problematic, this appears to be an unintended consequence of what they wrote. It is not surprising, therefore, that here we find yet another reason why a number of modern theologians have thought it worthwhile to pursue alternatives to Chalcedon.[83]

CONCLUSION

We are now in a position to return to an earlier observation. Contemporary christology is in crisis because the great affirmations of classic christological doctrine have themselves become questionable. Specifically, it is no longer apparent whether and how documents like the Nicene Creed and the Chalcedonian Definition effectively may inform contemporary Christian faith. In the absence of some of its main traditional points of reference, contemporary christological discourse lacks coherence. The field seems open not only to the creative but also to the eccentric and the bizarre. One therefore is tempted to observe that today "anything goes," and justifiably so, since the classical tradition of the Christian community has failed to deliver an intelligible and enduring frame of reference.

Before one casts Chalcedon aside, however, it seems important to ask just how we are to interpret the significance of its celebrated definition in the first place. The criticisms offered during the modern period reject the two-natures doctrine as a univocal specification of how humanity and divinity are united in Christ's person. At the same time, however, they tend to assume, at least implicitly, the correctness of Chalcedon's symbolic intent to insist upon a profound mystery, namely that Jesus Christ is decisive for how we are to envision both God and human life appropriately related to God. The fundamental objection is that the inherited formulas are not adequate to preserve the meaning that they themselves intended. Otherwise, why decry the difficulties that the two-natures doctrine erects to envisioning Jesus' true humanity and God's participation in his last sufferings? So we have reached an impasse. On the one hand, a number of modern theologians reject Chalcedon's two-natures doctrine as a univocal specification of how humanity and divinity coinhere in Jesus Christ. On the other hand, many of these same critics appear to affirm the essential mystery to which Chalcedon attests.

It may be that this very impasse supplies an important clue to a constructive estimate of Chalcedon's accomplishment. The history of the council as well as the developments leading up to it indicate that, by a confluence of ecclesiastical and imperial exigencies, the fathers were led to adopt a formula that plainly overextended their dialectical resources. It was tolerably clear, of course, that the definition's revolutionary vocabulary ruled out a number of then-popular accounts of the incarnation. But the definition's precise positive significance remained obscure. Indeed, it seems fair to say that, by rigorous philosophical standards, the definition represented a kind of fractured doctrine from the very first, one that employed terms such as *physis* and hypostasis more as symbols to point beyond themselves toward a mystery than as technical concepts to proffer a genuine explanation.

One may therefore justifiably regard Chalcedon as a symbolic state-ment that points toward the mystery of Jesus Christ and gives direction to subsequent attempts to speak about and envision Jesus, God, and man. One may believe, in short, that the symbolic intent of the two-natures doctrine is both more valuable and more fundamental than its metaphysical conceptuality.

Even when the definition is interpreted in this fashion, there is sufficient diversity in the New Testament to render implausible the contention that Chalcedon represents a necessary development of what we find there. It can and ought to be affirmed, however, that the Chalcedonian Definition represents a possible and appropriate devel-opment in meaningful continuity with what we find in the New Testament. Specifically, and despite the substantive metaphysical dif-ficulties, Chalcedon may be regarded as an attempt to secure the decisiveness of Jesus Christ in the context of the Hellenistic world. It presents a symbolic interpretation, in the terms of a fractured meta-physic, of the New Testament consensus on the centrality of Jesus Christ for our experience and understanding of God and of human life in appropriately responsive relation to God. Chalcedon develops this consensus in a specific direction under the pressure of particular challenges. So to say that the two natures are here united without separation or confusion and "without transmuting one nature into another" is to maintain that, in Jesus Christ, we really do come to apprehend both of these realities, that the reality of God is not to be collapsed into the reality of authentic human life or vice versa, and that knowledge of Jesus Christ is not knowledge of some third reality.

From this vantage point, one may regard the Chalcedonian Def-inition much as Athanasius regarded the Nicene Creed, namely, as a signpost against heresies.[84] It protected the New Testament consensus about the centrality of Jesus Christ when that consensus was threatened in the Hellenistic environment. Thus, many of the christological her-esies appear as challenges to the apprehension that Jesus Christ is decisive for both knowledge of the reality of God and knowledge of human life in authentic relation to God. Most ancient forms of adop-tionism denied that Jesus Christ is decisive for our apprehension of the reality of God. Docetism denied that Jesus Christ is decisive for our apprehension of genuinely human life. Apollinarianism, Arianism, and probably also Eutychianism entailed both deficiencies due to their tendencies to affirm that Jesus Christ is some third thing, other than either God or man.

Therefore, the Chalcedonian Definition may be interpreted as the culmination of a historical development that makes an intelligible affirmation about the centrality of Jesus Christ. The relationship that this affirmation upholds between Jesus Christ and our apprehensions of the reality of God and of human life in appropriate relation to God is the essential meaning and mystery of the orthodox tradition about Christ's person. Part of our constructive task is to recast the centrality of Jesus Christ in language that is informed by the symbolism of the classical formulas but not shackled by their metaphysical terms.

The christology that I develop in the following chapters will be informed by these conclusions. I will not attempt to reconstruct the problematic two-natures doctrine. As a consequence, my conceptuality will not lend itself to easy equivalence with the ontological terms of the conciliar formulas; nor will it be possible simply to read my proposal back into the field of options presented in past debates. Instead, I shall attempt to preserve the symbolic intent of the classical tradition by rendering both the centrality and the particularity of Jesus Christ, by means of an anthropology that emphasizes the importance of affectivity for personal identity.

Clearly, my interpretation does not retrieve *all* that Chalcedon probably meant in the minds of its framers. The definition long since has lost its significance as a compromise document that fleetingly promised the ecclesiastical peace so ardently sought by the imperial authorities of the fifth century. More importantly, for many of the fathers at Chalcedon, the doctrine of the two natures and one hypostasis not only meant that Jesus Christ is central but also laid an ontological foundation for redemption understood as a process of divinization. This foundation is not protected by nonmetaphysical interpretations of Chalcedon's meaning. Nevertheless, I have tried to keep a wider whole in view. An interpretation of Chalcedon as a statement of the centrality of Jesus Christ avoids many of the signal difficulties raised by modern critics, and also is compatible with the Reformation emphasis on the particularity of the atonement and on redemption as participation in Christ's victory over sin. If what I now interpret the definition to mean to the ongoing community of the church is not identical with what it likely meant to those who produced it, then at least there is a historical chain of connection between my present interpretation and what the definition originally meant. According to my interpretation, Chalcedon secures the decisive centrality of Jesus Christ, while later reflections about Christ's work secure his particularity. Chalcedon tells us *that* Jesus Christ is central. Later schematizations of Christ's work order the principal and particular features of what he says, does, and endures.

As we have seen, a number of writers construe the meaning of what Jesus Christ says, does, and endures in terms of either a twofold or threefold pattern; the images and their arrangements vary. Yet regardless of which pattern predominates in a given text, the triple functions of instruction-example, governance-guidance, and sacrifice-atonement are nearly always present in the fuller compass of an author's reflections. Thus, one may be informed by this tradition in one's contemporary reflections about what Jesus Christ says, does, and endures without being confined to a specific formulation or set of images. The essential point, and one that my christology of the heart aims to preserve, is that the Christian community's apprehension of Jesus Christ has a particularity about it, a kind of symbolic form, shape, or pattern. This apprehension is not exhausted by the conviction *that* we discern divine reality in Jesus Christ and *that* we discern human life as it should be related to God in Jesus Christ. Rather, our apprehension of Jesus Christ is patterned and its symbolic texture tells us what sort of reality God is and what sort of human life is genuinely responsive to divine reality. Moreover, this pattern, texture, or form exhibits a double character that parallels the centrality of Christ secured by the early councils. In what he says, does, and endures, Jesus Christ "is understood as man, perfectly directed toward God as his end, or perfectly obedient to the Father; and he is acknowledged as divine, as the power of God or as act or Word of God that redirects men who had lost their relation to their end." [85]

In my judgment, the centrality and particularity of Jesus Christ belong together. They are indispensable to the biblical witness as well as to the subsequent tradition of the church. They express the same object in the life of the Christian community. Christians do not know the pattern of Christ's action and endurance apart from the reality of God and of human life in appropriate relation to God; nor do they know in Christ the reality of God and of human life in appropriate relation to God apart from the particular form of Christ's action and endurance. In this sense, the particular figure of Jesus Christ remains the decisive focal point for the Christian vision of God and of humanity's place in God's world. Here, in the life of the Christian community, true divinity and true humanity intersect, and here they come to their true articulation.

3

Jesus Christ and the
New Testament

Someone who really belongs in his heart to the world of Christian
experience . . . will . . . insist upon standing with this symbol
on the solid ground of real life. It is for him a truly significant
fact that a real man thus lived, struggled, believed and conquered.
—Ernst Troeltsch

For a christology informed by classical Christianity, the centrality and particularity of Jesus Christ belong together. Indeed, their
interplay is crucial. Jesus Christ is decisive for the Christian community's apprehensions of God and human life in responsive relation
to God, and these apprehensions receive specific form and content
from the particulars of what Jesus Christ says, does, and endures.
Therefore, a task of Christian theology is to probe the reality of Jesus
Christ and so identify a symbolic form or pattern that indicates what
sort of reality God is and what sort of human life is genuinely responsive to God.

In another time, one might have proceeded directly from this
observation toward a constructive interpretation. Today, however,
biblical scholarship presents a critical difficulty. We cannot regard the
portraits of Jesus in the New Testament as strictly accurate historical
reports. The controlling interest of the New Testament writers was
to interpret the meaning of Jesus Christ for the early Christian communities rather than to proffer simple accounts of what happened.
Before we ask about a specific symbolic pattern that is provided by
the reality of Jesus Christ, we must ask whether the New Testament
furnishes sufficiently reliable access to any such pattern at all.

A CHALLENGE

It was just at this point that Albert Schweitzer's *The Quest for the Historical Jesus* exposed something of the over-confidence of liberal theology during the nineteenth century. Jesus, Schweitzer argued, cut a historical figure considerably more eschatological and elusive than many liberals had imagined. As a historical person, said Schweitzer, Jesus "remains a stranger to our time" and we can rely only on his words to communicate his spirit to us.[1] Critical theology therefore must operate with a different and more slender christological pattern.

This line of thinking is reflected in the work of one of the most influential New Testament theologians of the twentieth century. According to Rudolf Bultmann, one may affirm the "that" of Jesus' historical existence, that is, the outlines of his message and some events in his life. However, the "that" is an insufficient basis on which to reconstruct Jesus' manner of living. Instead, it is the *message* of Jesus that forms the presupposition for New Testament theology, and this message is an essentially eschatological proclamation of God's kingdom. " 'Now the time is come! God's Reign is breaking-in! The end is here!' "[2]

The New Testament, says Bultmann, does not repeat the message uttered by Jesus. Instead, it proclaims "Jesus Christ the Crucified and Risen One—to be God's eschatological act of salvation."[3] We therefore must reckon with a troubling disjunction between the historical Jesus and the message of the New Testament, where "the proclaimer became the proclaimed."[4] Nevertheless, a critical measure of continuity remains between the message of Jesus and that of the New Testament. Jesus' message of the in-breaking of God's kingdom confronted his hearers with a radical decision for or against obedience to God, and the biblical proclamation of Jesus Christ as God's decisive act of salvation confronts us with this same decision. One experiences a crisis of decision when confronted with the radical demand for obedience to God as it comes through in the kerygmatic proclamation of the New Testament.[5]

Thus, Bultmann squarely faces the fact that we cannot regard the portraits of Jesus in the New Testament as critically accurate history. Perhaps more importantly, he reminds us that there is considerably more at issue in christology than empirical fact claims. The

New Testament presents a decisive revelation of God and a decisive possibility for human life in appropriate relation to God. It speaks to people with power. There is a crucial connection between the New Testament message about Jesus Christ and the self-understanding of believers that is lost if one reduces christology to a historical investigation of the life and times of Jesus of Nazareth.

Nevertheless, Bultmann's position makes it extraordinarily difficult to retrieve the particularity of Jesus Christ. True, he insists upon the "that" of Jesus' existence. But this is hardly sufficient. How are we to comprehend what sort of divine demand and what sort of possibility for personal life have been mediated to us by a mere "that"? Indeed, one might expect both the divine demand and personal possibility to have some describable features or characteristics. Yet here we are left with a bald demand and a bare possibility for indeterminate obedience. A decisive demand and possibility for personal life have emerged with a definite individual, but we now have virtually no access to the pattern, style, or way of life with which they originally were connected.

Perhaps we should affirm that it is precisely this lack of form which frees Christians from all legalism or slavish adherence to predetermined patterns, thereby enabling them to remain open to the demand of God in the present. But the consequences of this affirmation for any distinctive contribution of christology either to the doctrine of God or to Christian ethics are extreme indeed. We can put little flesh on the bones of God's transcendence, and we can identify no pattern or form to the divine demand except to say that it is radical. Correspondingly, there is no general content or direction to be received from Jesus Christ other than the rather vague counsel not to live out of our own resources but to remain open to the divine demand in every moment.

Bultmann's notion of the decision that is constantly demanded by God and constantly has to be made by human agents does little more than affirm that the nature and content of the demand and obedience are left open; they become specific only in the concrete moment of decision. In general, God and human agency can be characterized only by self-determining freedom. We have no way to fill out materially *what* is demanded by God and *what* the decision is to which one is summoned. God takes no shape or form, just as human agency takes no shape or form. This formlessness emerges because Bultmann will not generalize about either God's demand or our obedience to it. One might expect christology to be of help at just this point, to furnish some indication of the form of God's demand and the form of our appropriate response. Instead, however, we find only the proclaimer of God's decisive eschatological demand, who is himself now proclaimed as God's decisive demand.

Clearly, Bultmann wishes to uphold the centrality of Jesus Christ, but he is unable to retrieve an adequate specification of the particularity of Jesus Christ. The result is that the particulars of what Jesus Christ does and endures are unable to contribute significant material specification to the apprehensions of God and of human life in responsive relation to God. That is, in the absence of a sufficiently rich and nuanced depiction of the particularity of Jesus Christ, his decisive centrality is rendered formless if not entirely vacuous.

By contrast, Bultmann's contemporary, Karl Barth, is concerned to represent the freedom of God as well as self-determining human agency; yet Barth makes stronger claims about the shape of God's command and the shape of human agency within the divine-human relationship. Neither God nor human being remains blank paper. In Jesus Christ, God discloses God's self as "the almighty Lord who wills what is best for the man who is responsible to him, who seeks his own glory by being man's Savior."[6] Here too, the human being is characterized as God's obedient covenant partner. God is the human being's Creator, Reconciler, and Redeemer. Accordingly, the human being is always creature, sinner, and child of God. Within this covenantal relationship, then, the divine–human encounter is articulated and differentiated. It receives general form.[7]

Barth counsels human beings to remain open to God's continuing actions, yet he is also concerned to identify an instructive pattern or skein. Under the impact of grace, human action receives the form, disposition, or attitude of the invocation of the gracious God. The Christian life is not one in which a person looks to his or her own resources, but one in which a person calls upon God in freedom, conversion, faith, gratitude, and faithfulness.[8] Correspondingly, Barth also maintains that law is a form of grace and that the Gospel portraits of Jesus do indeed provide guidance for the Christian life. He does not construct unexceptionable rules on this basis; to do so would be, in Barth's view, to restrict the freedom of God's living command. But he does insist that the grace disclosed in Jesus Christ has a particular shape, and that it requires Christians to do something distinctive, that is, "follow Jesus." Thus, just as God's sovereign freedom takes on a general pattern, so also the freedom that comes to us in Jesus Christ "takes place in a definite form and direction."[9] For Barth,

> The truth is . . . that what the Gospel sayings about the following of His disciples really preserve are certain prominent lines along which the concrete obedience always moved in relation to individuals, characterizing it as His commanding in distinction from that of other lords.[10]

These prominent lines in Jesus' commanding offer guidance having to do with service, possessions, the use of force, and so on.[11]

Thus, unlike Bultmann, Barth is able to specify the particularity of Jesus Christ and to pursue a line of thinking that is more firmly in accord with the classical Christian tradition. The particulars of what Jesus says, does, and endures make a decisive contribution to a differentiated portrait of God, and these same particulars make a decisive contribution to a differentiated characterization of human agency in covenantal relation with God. The interplay between the centrality and particularity of Jesus Christ is maintained, and this enables Barth to fill out materially both the shape of the divine command and the shape of human agency.

Again unlike Bultmann, however, Barth takes no clear account of modern research into the life of Jesus. Instead, he maintains that the "alien standards" of disciplines like history have little or no place in Christian dogmatics except as they are themselves made subject to the Word of God in Jesus Christ.[12] In this sense, Barth's theology remains noncritical. We therefore have no indication that the christological particulars to which Barth makes decisive appeals in his theology are congruent with the Jesus of history. True, we can be certain that they have a basis in Barth's reading of New Testament literature, but their actual dwelling place in the historical reality of Jesus of Nazareth is left unaddressed.

This brings us to a crossroads. Must we, in effect, choose either (with Bultmann) historical integrity at the cost of the particularity of Jesus Christ or (with Barth) the particularity of Jesus Christ at the cost of historical integrity? That question is worth pondering, since it presents, with reference to a specific problem, the more general challenge of what it means to stand in a living tradition. For if this really is our only choice, then classic christological doctrine, with its insistence upon the interplay between the centrality and the particularity of Jesus Christ, really does present a most troubling framework for contemporary reflection. If this really is our only choice, then the attempt to remain faithful to the guiding pattern of classical christology and, at the same time, to engage the intellectual challenges of the present world surely must fail.

My own judgment is that this challenge can be met, that we can retrieve the particularity of Jesus Christ without neglecting critical questions about the Jesus of history. This is because recent studies having to do with the interface between "nature and nurture" or biology and cultural history yield new perspectives on human behavior. When combined with commonly accepted outlines of the life of Jesus as well as literary studies of how biblical narratives portray character, these new perspectives allow us to offer a fresh appraisal of the relationship between the Jesus of history and the portraits of Jesus in the New Testament. Thus, in the course of the following argument, we shall journey to what surely will seem the far country of interdisciplinary reflections—*not* to emerge with significantly different evidence about the historical Jesus than is commonly accepted, but rather to establish a different way of interpreting the significance of commonly accepted evidence. The argument can be stated in four theses.

Thesis 1. Human subjectivity comes to significant expression in patterns of behavior.

This point is basic to the anthropology that underlies my constructive position as a whole, not only here but also in the following chapters. However, it is also somewhat controversial. For one thing, there is evidence that important reaches of human personality remain largely unconscious, and it is likely that these receive only partial and oblique expressions in behavior. Still, not all of human personality remains unconscious. There are desires, dispositions, and devotions of which we are at least partly aware. For example, parents are generally aware of their love for their children, and business executives are often aware of their desires for corporate advancement and success. To some degree, these too are borne unconsciously, yet they also emerge as conscious affectivities and commitments. My thesis is that these more or less conscious dimensions of our personalities come to significant expression in patterns of behavior.

Even at this level, significant difficulties attend all attempts to infer anything with confidence about a person's subjectivity. We generally do not assume that everything we hear a person say and see him do is an entirely accurate or full expression of his subjectivity. Moreover, people may falsely represent themselves. Schubert Ogden makes these points by quoting Søren Kierkegaard and then appealing to Paul: " 'For a lie can be stretched precisely as far as the truth—in the eyes of men, but not in the sight of God' "; so, "even 'if I give away all I have and if I deliver my body to be burned,' the possibility remains that I 'have not love.' "[13]

True enough; it is possible that Jesus was a liar, and that what his followers heard and saw of him actually represents their experience of a charade that they mistakenly regarded as evidence of his personal integrity. Again, it is possible that his earliest followers fundamentally misconstrued the relationship between Jesus' behavior and his commitments. For that matter, it is possible that what we see and hear of anyone is similarly unreliable. There are always risks when we dare to draw inferences about others. Still, the fact remains that, very often, we take these risks—particularly in the absence of contrary evidence; and, of course, contrary evidence is also subject to the same qualifications. The argument that we cannot draw credible inferences about someone's subjectivity in light of what we hear that person say and see that person do is really a celebration of radical doubt in our knowledge of people. Unless we are content to remain agnostic about everyone's subjectivity, then we have little choice but to assume some congruence between a person's commitments and what he or she says and does. Complete lack of confidence in our knowledge of people is practically untenable, if not also pathological.

Of course, we need to do more than attend to particulars; we need also to seek their unity. This is why we rarely believe that we

```
THE CAMPUS BOOK STORE
3406 BROOK ROAD
RICHMOND, VA 23227
(804) 353-6815
RESOURCES FOR MINISTRY


20204            A 10/06/89  4:04

3439   1*JESUS CHRIST &    9.85      9.85

            SUB-TOTAL              9.85
            TAX                     .00
            TOTAL                  9.85
            Cash -SALE
            AMT TENDERED          10.00

            CHANGE DUE              .15

THANK YOU
```

know someone after a single encounter. We look instead for *patterns* of behavior that appear characteristic. Once we apprehend these patterns in persons' behavior, then we gain some confidence that we know them, because we assume that these patterns are expressive of their wants, desires, devotions, and loyalties, and of the ways in which they typically prioritize them or give them order. We take this knowledge of others into account in our subsequent interactions and converse with them, and we adjust our beliefs about the sort of people they are in light of our continuing experience.

Why do we go through all this? Partly, no doubt, because we are naturally curious about other people. This is one reason why gossip is a popular pastime. But also because nothing less than this seems required if we are to build and sustain meaningful and dependable social relationships.

That, in short, is a common-sensical defense of the contention that human subjectivity comes to expression in human behavior and that we justifiably, though not uncritically, rely on perceived patterns of behavior to tell us something about the sorts of persons we encounter. We do not really understand someone until we are able to connect relatively persistent features of his or her behavior with certain affections, dispositions, desires, and devotions.

A defense of this contention need not rely on common sense alone. Recent work in evolutionary biology and ethology also suggests a connection between affection and action as a useful hypothesis for understanding behavior. "We are in fact so constituted," writes Mary Midgley, "that we cannot act at all if feeling really fails."[14] Significantly, our feelings or affections are not chaotic but are formed into specific configurations—what Midgley refers to as our "emotional constitutions" and what much classical literature calls our hearts.

Our hearts are responsive to a variety of influences and conditions in their formation, and are expressive of their particular configurations or formations in patterns of action. They are responsive to their genetic foundations and come to expression in certain species-specific patterns of action.[15] This can be seen if we attend to the fact that certain kinds of behavior are almost universally present among humans, and that this is true also of other animals. Beavers build dams. Buffalo roam. People form families, live in groups, communicate, and strive for social recognition. Generally, these animals do these things rather than other things, and they do them partly because they are predisposed to do them by their genetically funded emotional constitutions.[16]

Among the higher social animals, emotional constitutions also are responsive in their formation and expression to influences and conditions in the social environment. Dispositions in humans are especially responsive to culture and society. A social environment is a way of awakening our faculties and shaping our dispositions or affections.[17] Our dispositions are responsive in their formation and expression to our culture, its symbols and values, and the ways these orient us toward activities in the arts, sciences, politics, economics, religion, and so forth. Again, our emotional constitutions are responsive in their formation and expression to our society, both in its structures of patterned activity and association, and in more personal encounters. There is interplay among biological and social factors in the formation and expression of our emotional constitutions; we need not choose between "nature" and "nurture."[18]

So it happens that many people may be genetically endowed with special aptitudes for music, but few are suitably disposed toward becoming accomplished musicians. This is partly because whether one is encouraged to pursue music as a vocation, and precisely what sort of music one is encouraged to make, depends largely upon one's social environment. It is a matter of luck, and comes from outside.[19] Among other things, then, Ludwig von Beethoven's disposition toward musical accomplishment was responsive in its formation and expression to inherent genius, structured opportunities for training, tutelage under a specific master (Franz Josef Haydn), and the strong value placed upon a certain sort of musical excellence in Viennese high culture. Indeed, one investigator uses Beethoven as an illustration of the need for social recognition, and points out that this need rendered Beethoven especially responsive to the recognition accorded musical genius in Vienna. According to Joseph Lopreato, the need for recognition was strong enough in Beethoven largely to overpower the desires for family life that often qualify the drive for vocational excellence.[20]

Significantly, a concentration on disposition or affection does not leave the mind out of account. Heart and mind, affect and intellect are complementary. An appropriate understanding of their interrelation indicates that our emotional constitutions also are responsive in their formation and patterned expressions to individual deliberation and decision.

Because they frequently come into conflict, our biologically funded and socially formed desires and dispositions need to be organized. This is especially so the more complex and elastic an animal's emotional constitution is, and among those animals whose social environments present varied possibilities. Reason is a name for organizing oneself, for arranging feelings and desires, and for resolving conflicts between them. People have integrating centers to their personalities, and rationality as integration is closely bound to "having a character."[21]

Consider a married woman in contemporary America who is confronted with important choices about having children and pursuing her career. If she is like many women, she has strong desires to raise children of her own. There are biological reasons for this, and the future of the human species would be rendered precarious indeed were it not generally the case. Her husband also possesses a genetically funded emotional constitution that predisposes him toward wanting and caring for children, but it is no use claiming that his and hers are the same. Significantly, her desires also have been formed or drawn out in certain directions by her social environment, by the symbols of womanhood current in the culture, by her experience of social structures like the family, and by her personal encounters with parents and friends.

As a member of a highly social species, it is likely that our protagonist also shares with the rest of us genetically based needs for social communication and recognition that may not be met by the isolated situation of a mother at home in a modern residential neighborhood. It is probable, moreover, that these needs will be responsive to the high value placed upon gainful employment in our culture. They are likely also to be responsive to her experiences of certain educational institutions, employment situations, and social companions.

The limited variety of options presented by American society calls for a choice, and our protagonist will need to engage in two related lines of reasoning if she is to integrate her affections with the available possibilities. She will need to consult her desires, and she will need to consider the consequences of adopting one or another course of action.

She needs to consult her desires. Is either so strong that it largely overpowers the other? If so, she may decide against having children and devote herself instead to her career. Or, she may give up all prospects of a career in order to have and raise children. For many women, however, neither desire will predominate so strongly as to render either of these radical choices appropriate. If our protagonist is one of these women, she is stuck with a genuine dilemma, and may well consider certain "intermediate" courses of action such as the following, their feasibility and consequences:

● She might stay home to raise her children and then return to her career following a significant leave.

● She might stay home following the birth of each child, engage the services of a day-care provider, and continue her career with moderate leaves.

● She might engage the services of a day-care provider on a part-time basis and continue to work outside of her home part-time until she thinks her children are old enough for her to return to full-time employment.

● She might combine any of these options with a reduction in the time that her husband spends working outside of their home so that he also can provide a significant share of day care.

Obviously, the feasibility of these options depends on a number of things: the willingness of employers to make provisions for maternity and paternity leaves; part-time employment or reductions in workloads for parents with young children; re-entry training and guarantees that a parent who has been at home caring for children will be able to resume employment in a position comparable to the one he or she left; a husband who is willing to modify his career goals in order to be at home with his children; and so forth. All of the options require that the financial burden of reduced or suspended employment for one or both parents can be borne by the family.

The main point I want to make here, however, is that, within the limits of what is feasible, each option represents an ordering or integration of certain conscious features of our protagonist's emotional constitution. Each represents a kind of integrative balance of affectivity because each pattern allows a certain affective balance to come to expression. In this sense, our emotional constitutions are responsive in both their formation and expression to the choices we make. Our decisions have something to do with the sorts of persons we become, and we become who we are partly by pursuing particular courses of action. If, then, our protagonist chooses to stay at home to raise her children and then return to her career, this pattern of behavior reflects a certain integrative balance of wants and desires, or what is in her heart and on her mind. To understand our protagonist both sympathetically and adequately, it will be necessary to consider her pattern of behavior in light of her desires and commitments both to raise her children and to pursue her career. We shall not really understand her until we are able to connect her behavioral patterns with certain affections and devotions.

In summary, both common sense and recent studies support the contention that human subjectivity comes to expression in patterns of behavior and that we justifiably, although not uncritically, rely on perceived patterns of behavior to tell us something about the sorts of persons we encounter. An agent's behavioral patterns reflect affections, his or her devotions, commitments, dispositions, desires, and intentions. They also reflect his or her choices and deliberations. Many of these are formed or drawn out in socially and historically particular ways from a biological base. Their specific configuration or balance represents a confluence of nature and nurture that sets an individual's practical orientation, stance, or character. To know someone is to grasp this balance and the often subtle and delicate relationship between inner and outer, subjectivity and action.

Here, of course, we are interested primarily in Jesus Christ, someone we do not know apart from the texts of the New Testament. And this raises the question of how the Gospels furnish the reader with access to the character of their principal human figure.

Thesis 2. The Gospel narratives disclose the character of Jesus Christ by portraying key connections between his subjectivity and his behavior.

The Gospels are narratives. By this I mean that they present sequential stories in the voices of narrators. Moreover, they are narratives concerned with characterization, and that focus upon the life, ministry, death, and resurrection of Jesus Christ. No doubt they have other interests too, for instance, witnessing to the resurrection and proclaiming Jesus Christ as God's decisive revelation. But they pursue none of these apart from portrayals of the character of Jesus Christ, or the relation between his subjectivity and his behavior.

In general, my understanding of how narratives reveal character follows from the argument above about subjectivity. If heart and mind come to expression in patterns of behavior, then narratives may do more than rehearse words and deeds. They may also display unitive patterns of particular words and deeds and thereby suggest the inward subjectivity that is congruent with or accompanies the external particulars. In sum, narratives may depict "the unity of the particulars and the inward of the externals."[22]

One way that some narratives do this is by displaying significant correspondences between what a person says and does. Moreover, the more illuminating narratives in this regard often are not those that list everything someone said or did. When it comes to characterization, selection is a key narrative strategy precisely because pattern is paramount. Good storytellers know this. The more effective narrative portrayals of an agent are often those that, by selectively presenting only certain things a person said and did in certain contexts, are able to represent the characteristic features that disclose the person.

When, for example, in George Meredith's *The Egoist,* the very eligible bachelor, Willoughby Patterne, declares his love for Clara Middleton, but then goes on to treat both her and their engagement as little more than evidence of his own attractiveness and worth, we have reason to doubt that his declaration furnishes us with a reliable access to his innermost feelings. Meredith is trying to tell us that Willoughby may say lots of things, but he is incapable of loving anyone other than himself. By contrast, however, when Herman Melville's Ahab in *Moby Dick* declares on the quarterdeck that he would smite the sun if it

offended him, and then feverishly pursues his maniacal, self-destruc-
tive quest for the great white whale, we justifiably regard his statement
as one that accurately reflects his inward passion.

On balance, with respect to characterization, the portraits of
Jesus in the Gospels are more like Melville's Ahab than Meredith's
Willoughby. There are, for example, important correspondences between Jesus' teachings and his behavior. If Jesus teaches his followers
to love their enemies, he also heals the centurion's servant and breaks
bonds of prejudice by speaking with a Samaritan woman. If he preach-
es a message of repentance and forgiveness, he also sits at the table
with tax collectors and sinners. If he teaches love of God, he is also
obedient to God, even unto death on a cross. The effect of these
correspondences is to disclose something of Jesus' person, his dominant devotion, dispositions, attitudes, and intentions.

There are other ways that a narrator may attempt to reveal character. For example, one of the heights of biography is when, after
having portrayed a number of the subject's relevant actions and words
as well as the impressions these have made upon others, the biographer
is able to draw a central inference about the subject's character. Here,
for instance, is a passage from William McFeeley's recent biography
of Ulysses S. Grant:

> The problem was that he was frightened of intimacy with people
> on the other side of the tracks. In such a relationship, their dis-
> comfort would have been momentary . . . they would have re-
> laxed when they found that he was not a man of pretensions. The
> source of his discomfort, on the other hand, was far more deeply
> seated. . . . He was afraid of falling back. Seeing groups of or-
> dinary people brought reminders of the possibility of failure—
> and failure frightened him. He could not allow it to return and
> engulf him.[23]

Here, the narrator uses direct statements about the agent's subjectivity
to communicate a generalization that might escape a mere ledger of
particulars. The passage helps to convey character and to portray a
person just because it risks an interpretation of an inward passion that
accompanied Grant in so many of his acts of greatness and smallness,
engagement and withdrawal.

The Gospels do not share the critical interests of many modern biographies. Moreover, by comparison with most modern narratives, the style of the Gospels is remarkably sparse. Nowhere, for example, do we find as extended a statement about a character's subjectivity as in the above quotation from McFeeley's *Grant*. Yet the Gospels do employ the technique of direct statement about general features of their protagonist's subjectivity in connection with his words and deeds. So, after having given an account of the beginning of Jesus' ministry ("Repent, for the kingdom of heaven is at hand," Matt. 3:17), the Sermon on the Mount, and a number of Jesus' healings, the narrator of the Gospel of Matthew makes a transition to an important statement about discipleship with these sentences:

> And Jesus went about all the cities and villages, teaching in their synagogues and preaching the gospel of the kingdom, and healing every disease and every infirmity. When he saw the crowds, he had compassion for them, because they were harassed and help-less, like sheep without a shepherd. Then he said to his disciples, "The harvest is plentiful, but the laborers are few; pray therefore the Lord of the harvest to send out laborers into his harvest" (9:35–38).

The almost-passing remark that "he had compassion for them" is the narrator's direct statement about Jesus' attitude in conjunction with his ministry. The passage as a whole connects this attitude with loyalty to God and some central images of discipleship. A disciple, then, is like a shepherd or like a laborer working to bring in the harvest. Like the master, the disciple is one who goes teaching, preaching, and heal-ing to all the cities and towns with compassion for the harassed and helpless. Thus, the narrator endeavors to portray an inward passion in connection with Jesus' ministry and to recommend it to Jesus' fol-lowers.

While the interposition of direct statements about an agent's sub-jectivity is one of the most obvious means of narrative characterization, it is hardly the only way that a narrator can attempt to portray an agent as a complex of motive and feeling. Robert Alter, in his illu-minating book on *The Art of Biblical Narrative,* points out that dialogue is another important tool. In addition,

> Character can be revealed through the report of actions; through appearance, gestures, posture, costume; through one character's

comments on another; through direct speech, either summarized or quoted as interior monologue; or through statements by the narrator about the attitudes and intentions of the personages, which may come either as flat assertions or motivated explanations.[24]

It is worth dwelling for a moment on the wide variety of techniques available to a narrator who sets out to portray a character. All are ways of getting at the relation between the inward and the externals, and almost all appear at one time or another in the Synoptic Gospels.

More than a few are present in Mark's account of Jesus at Gethsemane (14:32–42). In verse 33, "began to be greatly distressed and troubled" is a statement by the narrator about Jesus' feelings. The point is powerfully reinforced in a manner that foreshadows the crucifixion by a bit of dialogue in verse 34, "And he said to them, 'My soul is very sorrowful, even unto death. . . .' " Jesus' prayer in verse 36 appears to be an example of narrative omniscience since, as we may surmise from the next verse, all potential witnesses are either drowsy or asleep. The words of the prayer, which we are told Jesus says at least twice—"Abba, Father, all things are possible to thee; remove this cup from me; yet not what I will, but what thou wilt"—form the centerpiece in a scene of passionate conflict. The conflict is focused all the more forcefully on Jesus alone by his going to Gethsemane with the disciples at night, progressively separating himself from them in order to pray, and periodically returning to find them asleep. The effect of all this is to portray Jesus as one who is profoundly tempted in the face of his fate, but who nevertheless inwardly consents to God's will. Finally, we should note also that even the sparest statement on the part of the protagonist, when it is delivered in poignant circumstances, may serve to disclose inward affection. A most powerful example is Luke's portrayal of Jesus' statement on the cross, "Father, forgive them" (23:24).

In my judgment, the Gospels are narratives that are constructed to portray, among other things, an agent's inward affections in relation to externals, and so to reveal a character and recommend a way of living. It will help to strengthen this point if we observe that some narratives are constructed so as to hide or obscure a character. For example, some of the stories in the Hebrew scriptures about David's emergence as a prominent leader intentionally convey profound uncertainty about his innermost feelings. The narrator in 1 Samuel employs a number of techniques to convey a sense of mystery about David's character, such as silence about David's feelings in some circumstances, studiously ambiguous statements about his feelings in other circumstances, and opaque dialogue. Most of these are connected with the general strategy of displacing access to David the private person by means of David the public man.[25]

All of this contrasts with the general tendency of the Gospel narratives, especially at key dramatic moments, to supply the reader with sharp access to Jesus' affections. With respect to the project of rendering character, then, some narratives are constructed to be opaque while others, like the Gospels, are disclosive. The difference between the two is whether a narrative aims at establishing reliable connections between a subject's affections and his or her external circumstances and behavior. Having concluded, then, that the Gospels are constructed so as to disclose the character of their chief protagonist, we need now to ask about the relationship between these narratives and the Jesus of history.

Thesis 3. There is a rough consensus about what Jesus was heard to have said and seen to have done by his earliest followers.

Ogden rightly notes that what we can reconstruct of the Jesus of history is never separate from the earliest testimonies of his followers: "Strictly speaking, all we can ever hope to talk about is not what Jesus said and did, but what Jesus was *heard* to have said and *seen* to have done by those on whose experience and memory of him we are utterly dependent.[26] Therefore, we cannot reconstruct a neutral portrait of Jesus as he was in himself, but only a portrait of how he seemed to be to interested parties. What is meant by "the Jesus of history," then, is the impression that the one called "Jesus of Nazareth" made upon others. We simply lack the sort of historical sources that might enable us to go further than this. Strictly speaking, however, this is all that is allowed by the evidence we have about a lot of people— my grandfather Albert, for instance. But not always; sometimes people leave written compositions from their own hands, for example, a set of letters as we have from Paul.

With this in mind, however, we should note that, while we are limited in what we can plausibly reconstruct of Jesus' life and ministry, a number of relevant points are not especially controversial. Jesus of Nazareth was baptized by John and may have been one of John's followers. He preached a prophetic message of repentance and the nearness of God's kingdom. His teaching, which emphasized radical devotion to God and love of neighbor, was in a measure of continuity with previous Jewish traditions, although it also departed from some of these traditions. He had followers, but he offended many. He associated with the poor and with outcasts. He was crucified by local authorities. All this is allowed even by Bultmann.[27]

To this sketch I am willing to add at least two things. First, the observed manner of Jesus' life and ministry was such that his followers ascribed to him a certain integrity. There was a perceived correspondence between what he said and what he did. Moreover, it reasonably may be inferred that the summaries of Jesus' words and deeds on which our sketch of relevant points is based represent summaries of relatively persistent patterns in Jesus' life and ministry in the experience of his followers. In their experience and memory, Jesus did not proclaim the kingdom just once; he did not teach love of God and neighbor just once; nor did he associate with the poor and the outcast only on a single occasion. Rather, he said and did these things with relative persistence. These points, then, may be regarded as patterns that Jesus' followers took to be disclosive of the sort of person he was. Second, the observed manner in which Jesus went to his crucifixion was such that many of his followers eventually interpreted his death to be of a piece with his life and ministry. Their memory was that Jesus' devotion to God and God's kingdom set him in opposition to local religious and political authorities. Moreover, their memory was not that Jesus railed against his fate or that he went kicking and screaming to the cross. Rather, their memory was that the way he went to the cross indicated that, at some level, he consented to his fate. These last two points go beyond what Bultmann allows, but not without good cause if we agree that, ordinarily, people do take a person's words and deeds as evidences of his or her subjectivity.[28]

Thesis 4. Jesus' manner of living as it is portrayed in the Gospels is congruent with the early witnesses' apprehension of his integrity.

When we turn to the New Testament, it is important to recognize that, while this diverse collection of literature does indeed proclaim Jesus Christ, it portrays him as one who points toward God and God's kingdom. Jesus' eschatological proclamation and his call to repentance are subject to a variety of interpretations in the Gospels, but they are not lost (e.g., Matt. 4:17; Mark 1:14). Again, although it is likely that the New Testament says considerably more about Jesus than he said about himself, this is exactly what one might expect. For if Jesus not only spoke but also embodied in his life the message that he uttered, then it makes sense that, in attempting to represent his significance, the Christian community should also proclaim the proclaimer. Indeed, it seems appropriate that the proclaimer's embodiment of his cause should have come to be represented through dramatic narratives or stories. It does not seem strange that the relationship between God and the one who bore a decisive message about and commitment to God should have become a matter of urgent concern to those who attempted to comprehend the significance of Jesus' life.

Finally, we should also note that the narrative portrayals and symbolic thematizations of Jesus and his message in the New Testament suggest other features that emerge in historical reconstructions of his life and ministry. The Gospels depict Jesus' baptism by John. The Christ of the New Testament both interprets and criticizes received Jewish traditions. He teaches love of God and neighbor, and he takes particular care to instruct his disciples. He is portrayed as a man of integrity whose teaching is reflected in his actions: in healing the sick; in associating with the poor, with tax collectors, and with sinners; and in delivering himself up to be crucified at the hands of local authorities.

In light of these considerations, it seems fair to endorse the general import of statements like the following one by Ernst Käsemann, who admits that the portraits of Jesus in the Gospels are not critically accurate and that the true history they do contain is overlaid with theological interpretation:

> In the Gospels as we have them there are decisive pivotal points which allow continuity to be established [between the Gospels and authentic history]. . . . They are grouped round Jesus' message of the gracious God, his critique—conditioned by this message and expressed both in word and work—of the law of Moses

and its interpretation, his radical demand for obedience and love,
and his death as the logical culmination of his ministry.[29]

Indeed, in my judgment, we must reckon with the fact that much of
what the New Testament portrays as historical occurrence actually
amounts to narrative and symbolic thematization that aims to display
the meaning of Jesus Christ for the early Christian communities. The
New Testament tends to present theological construals of the significance of Jesus Christ rather than historical reports. By means of narratives, metaphors, and summary statements about Jesus' life, ministry, death, and resurrection, the New Testament presents a symbolic
form rather than a biography. Even so, there are decisive points that
allow continuity to be established between this symbolic form and the
Jesus of history.

The question I should like to raise here is as follows. Can we,
in light of the decisive points of continuity between the New Testament
Christ and the historical Jesus, conclude that there is a connection
between the perceived integrity of the historical Jesus and the correspondence between his teaching and example that is portrayed in the
Gospels? Does it constitute a plausible interpretation of the significance
of Jesus' integrity to portray him as the Gospels do—in terms of a
correspondence of his teaching about God and God's kingdom and
about love of God and neighbor with things such as healing the sick;
casting out demons; having compassion on crowds; associating with
the poor, with tax collectors, and with sinners; delivering himself up
to be crucified; and praying that his executioners be forgiven?

We can reconstruct certain aspects of Jesus' message as well as
certain features of his life and ministry. We also know that his followers
ascribed to him a certain integrity, for they depicted a correspondence
between what he said and the way he acted or behaved. As we have
them, the Gospels do not represent critically accurate history so much
as theological construals and dramatic portrayals of the significance of
Jesus Christ for human life in relation to God. But there are decisive
points of continuity between the Gospels and what we can reconstruct
about the Jesus of history. These include points about his message as
well as general features of his behavior. The question is whether the
portrayal of Jesus' manner of living in the Gospels—via a correspondence between what he teaches (repentance, the nearness of God's kingdom, love of God and neighbor, and so on) and what he does (heal

the sick, cast out demons, associate with the poor and downtrodden, deliver himself up to be crucified)—represents a plausible interpretation of the significance of his historically perceived integrity. Remember that, in light of what we know about the historical Jesus, the perceived correspondence between what he said and what he did is quite likely to have involved correspondences between points in his teaching and behavior that are similar to some of the points portrayed in the Gospels. In my judgment, then, there is a measure of congruence between the historical figure of Jesus and the portraits of Jesus Christ in the Gospels.

CONCLUSION

The Gospels depict Jesus as one who, in some continuity with his cultural heritage and social environment, proclaims God and God's kingdom and exhibits certain patterns of behavior. It has been common in the longer theological tradition to regard many of these patterns as disclosive of formed dispositions or virtues; for instance, associating with outcasts and suffering reproach express humility.[30] They portray a manner of life or what is in Jesus' heart and on his mind. I agree in substance with Friedrich Schleiermacher and H. Richard Niebuhr that these virtues or dispositions and the patterns of activity in which they are expressed can be understood both sympathetically and adequately only in terms of Jesus' radical devotion and response to the mighty God of Israel. Many virtues come to expression in the New Testament portraits of Jesus' conduct and teaching. "But he practices none of them and requires none of them of his followers otherwise than in relation to God."[31] It is this center of confidence and loyalty that predominates in him and that forms the cornerstone for his personal balance or integrity. So, for example, in the Gospels, the patterned expressions in action of Jesus' emotional constitution that take the form of love are to be understood not only as responses to his neighbors and enemies, but also as responses that are shaped by his abiding loyalty and response to God. This balance comes through in the Gospels, and I see no compelling reason to think that it represents a cast of mind or temper of heart that is incongruous with what we know of the Jesus of history.

This line of thinking has a number of implications. First, it is a mistake to reduce the essential message of the New Testament to short kerygmatic formulae (e.g., born, died, buried, raised). The narrative portraits of Jesus Christ also are essential witnesses to the one who bore the new possibility for communion between God and human beings both in word and in deed. Not only what Bultmann calls kerygma, but also what one may call the fuller symbolic pattern of Jesus Christ portrayed by the Gospel narratives is integral for a Christian estimate of Jesus' significance. "This does not mean that the Gospels are biographies in the usual sense. They are proclamation; but the proclamation takes the form of a story of a man's life."[32]

Second, we need not drive a wedge between the Jesus of history, or the earliest stratum of Christian witnesses to him, and the Christ of the New Testament when it comes to specifying the subject of christological predicates. Indeed, to some extent, we never really have one without the other. This is a lesson to be learned from the quests for the Jesus of history; we never have Jesus apart from the Christian community and, for that community, Jesus and the Christ belong together. "For Christians it is at least as important to reject the thought that Jesus Christ is only an historical figure as it is to deny that he is only a symbol."[33]

Third, in meaningful continuity with the Jesus of history, the New Testament not only proclaims Jesus Christ as God's decisive work of redemption, but it also presents the symbolic form of Jesus Christ as one who embodies and teaches a particular manner of life that coheres with his orientation and commitment to God and God's reign. Therefore, our responses to the New Testament appropriately include our responses to a particular manner of living anchored in and balanced by radical devotion to God. The significance of this manner of life for those who believe that Jesus Christ is disclosive of God and of human life in relation to God is great indeed. As symbolic pattern or form, Jesus Christ becomes for Christians that special occasion that is able to elucidate all other occasions. He becomes a focal point or interpretative key for a vision of God and of human life in God's world. He becomes a pattern of passion, action, and endurance that is able to help form Christians in their orientations toward God and toward the world as God's dominion. Indeed, the ability of the New Testament portraits of Jesus Christ to elicit an orientation that lends direction and sense to life in God's world is one of the reasons why the New Testament is held in such high regard among Christians.

Although the Gospels do not present a critically accurate history, there are significant continuities between them and the Jesus of history. These continuities allow for specifications of the particularity of Jesus Christ that are both informed by biblical thematizations of Jesus' significance and congruent with admittedly sparse but nevertheless plausible reconstructions of his life and ministry. The New Testament furnishes interpretations of what Jesus says, does, and endures, which may lend form and content to our apprehensions of God and of human life in appropriate relation to God. Therefore, we need not choose between the particularity of Jesus Christ and attention to critical issues raised by modern historical scholarship. The way is clear intelligibly to retrieve the insistence of Christian tradition upon the interplay between the centrality and the particularity of Jesus Christ. Recent scholarship does not require that we abandon this classical enterprise; it rather demands that we exercise caution in framing the empirical claims that accompany our christological constructs. Christians may indeed stand with the originating pattern of Jesus Christ on the solid ground of real life.

4

The Truth, the Way,
and the Life

Why do you call him *Our Lord?*
Because, not with gold or silver but at the cost of his blood, he
has redeemed us body and soul from sin, and all the dominion
of the devil, and has bought us for his very own.
—The Heidelberg Catechism

The Christian vision of God and of human life in God's world
receives form and content from the particulars of what Jesus Christ
says, does, and endures as these are portrayed in the New Testament.
Jesus Christ discloses the contours of God's grace, purposes, and power
as well as the contours of the sort of human life that is genuinely
responsive to God. The particularity of Jesus Christ expresses a certain
balance or pattern that shapes the vision of God and man.

As we have seen, many classical interpretations of the particularity of Jesus Christ include three elements: teaching-instruction,
governance-guidance, and sacrifice-atonement. My interpretation is
also threefold, and can be stated as follows. Jesus Christ teaches the
truth about God's dominion and about human life in God's world. He
embodies a way of living that coheres with the truth, and so guides
or governs the Christian life. He empowers this life by his sacrifice
on the cross, and so enables sinners to walk in the way and to lead
lives in alignment with the truth. This interpretation attempts to summarize in a kind of symbolic shorthand the particular balance or pattern
of Jesus Christ. It tries to look at the figure of Jesus in a fashion that
illumines what it means to say that he is the Christ, the center of the

story of God's dealings with human beings, the decisive disclosure of God and of human life in relation to God.

Two further preparatory notes: first, just as the lines between the traditional metaphors of prophet, king, and priest are fluid and imprecise, so the images of the one who teaches the truth, embodies the way, and empowers the life are also approximate. At points they overlap. For example, Jesus teaches the truth not only in what he says but also by his active expression of the way of life that he embodies. My purpose, then, is not to draw precise distinctions, but rather to interpret a dynamic and differentiated whole, to lift up that multifaceted prism by which Christians envision God and man. Second, whereas traditional twofold and threefold symbolizations often treat Jesus' resurrection and victory over sin and death under the heading of his kingly or governing activity, I have reserved my interpretation of the significance of Jesus' resurrection until the end of my discussion. This is because I believe that an adequate understanding of the one who teaches the truth, embodies the way, and empowers the life forms the necessary condition for the Christian community's continuing experience of Jesus Christ as Lord and Savior. Without this understanding, the confession that "He is risen" is shorn of its particular content and power.

THE ONE WHO TEACHES THE TRUTH

Jesus teaches the truth. To say this is to affirm much of what Thomas Aquinas described as the function of communicating "the things of God" and what John Calvin meant by Christ's prophetic activity. It is to agree with Augustine that Jesus Christ teaches "the perfect measure of the Christian life." In biblical terms, it is to acknowledge what the Gospel writers were suggesting when they portrayed Jesus teaching with authority and claimed that others called him "Rabbi" or "Teacher."[1] Jesus Christ recapitulates God's way with Israel as it was expressed through the law and the prophets. He stands within this historical tradition as an innovator who at the same time confirms it. There can be little doubt that, for the writers of the New Testament and also many classical Christian theologians, Jesus is more than a teacher, a lawgiver, or a prophet. Yet it is equally certain that, for them, he is the one who teaches the truth and brings perfect wisdom.

There often has been a tendency to think that the image of teacher highlights Jesus' communication of particular moral rules and theological doctrines, but this is too narrow a view. Jesus' instruction in the New Testament takes a variety of forms, and much that he says fits neither the model of moral prescription nor that of formal doctrine (e.g., the Beatitudes and parables). It is important, therefore, to develop an understanding of the one who teaches the truth that is not confined to these forms.

For Christians, Jesus Christ teaches that the world is the realm of God's grace. It is a realm where God feeds birds and clothes lilies, though neither birds nor lilies labor. In less poetic terms, it is a realm in which God both brings into existence and sustains every creature. Therefore, it makes sense to ask this universal power for our daily bread. It is a realm of grace rather than merit, in which rain falls on the fields of the just and the unjust. It is a realm of grace rather than merit, within which people receive both gifts and impediments through no righteousness or fault of their own. It is an order within which we and all that we have are dependent on God.[2] One might observe that it is as much as if Jesus were saying to his followers that we are not our own, that the power which creates all things also faithfully sustains them, and so therefore it is appropriate to place one's confidence in that power and to address that power as "Father."[3]

This is one reason why to preach Jesus Christ is to proclaim release to captives and to preach good news to sinners, the downtrodden, the poor, and the sick. For one's relation to the God to whom Jesus points is not contingent upon one's social position, physical health, merits, or faults. Instead, the God whose world is a realm of grace stands in relation to all creatures without prejudice to these things. The question thrust before us by Jesus' teaching is not how one's social position, physical health, or moral performance can place one in relation to God, but whether we may come to acknowledge the gracious relationship in which God always already stands to us, and how our acceptance of God may be responsively reflected in our lives.

Indeed, this furnishes an essential clue to other dimensions of

Jesus' teaching. Jesus Christ is the one whose teaching both elicits and proclaims confidence in and loyalty to God as a dominant devotion that lends authentic orientation to human life in God's world. This devotion forms the center of weight or balance in Jesus' life and ministry. And, as has been frequently repeated in the theological tradition, it is indissolubly joined with the disposition to love one's neighbor, because loyalty to God entails loyalty to the creatures that God creates and upholds.[4] Our love of God finds in the Creator the one who points to creatures.[5]

The Gospels depict Jesus' insistence upon this connection, one that would appear to be central to the integrity of his manner of life, by joining two imperatives:

> And one of them, a lawyer, asked him a question to test him. "Teacher, which is the great commandment in the law?" And he said to him, "You shall love the Lord your God with all your heart, and with all your soul, and with all your mind. This is the great and first commandment. And a second is like it, You shall love your neighbor as yourself. On these two commandments depend all the law and the prophets" (Matt. 22:35–40; parallels Mark 12:28–34, Luke 10:25–37).

This passage has been interpreted in a variety of ways. Aquinas says that the injunction to love God is the principle in virtue of which one is to fulfill the precepts of charity toward others.[6] According to John Calvin, Matt. 22:35–40 and parallels indicate that the "foundation and structure of holy, upright living [is] the service of God and of men." The command to love the neighbor is like the first because, in order for people to love their neighbors, devotion to God must first displace their self-centeredness and inordinate self-concern.[7] Jonathan Edwards makes a similar point when he says that devotion to God overcomes the selfish spirit and thus turns the heart toward others. Therefore "love to God is the foundation of gracious love to men."[8] For those who follow Jesus, a dominant devotion to God becomes an orienting attitude or motive for the moral life because hearts and minds that are opened toward God are no longer centered exclusively upon themselves.

A number of Jesus' teachings amount to sayings that engender or recommend dispositions appropriately connected with and shaped by this dominant devotion. This is one way to understand some of the Beatitudes. "Blessed are the meek, for they shall inherit the earth" (Matt. 5:5). Meekness or humility is a disposition toward others that fits with a life oriented by devotion to God. It coheres with Jesus' teachings about God and God's order of grace, because humility is an appropriate disposition for those who acknowledge that they and all they are depend upon God. Moreover, humility goes together with gratitude because life is a gift. It goes together with praise and thanksgiving because that we are and who we are comprise our first debt. Again, humility is an appropriate disposition for those who acknowledge their sin before God and who recognize that all fall short of the kingdom and its glory. "Humility," says Augustine, "is part of our confession that we are sinners."[9]

This teaching is further confirmed by Christ's example. Hence Paul exhorts the Philippians to have the same mind (Calvin and others say this means the same attitude) that was in Christ. Humility takes the form of a servant in the life of the one "who emptied himself" and "who humbled himself and became obedient unto death." In Christ, Christians begin to see a great truth: Humility before God is indissolubly connected to our relations with others. By his words, deeds, and endurance, Jesus Christ recommends humility as an appropriate quality of discipleship, a disposition that inclines people in the mind of Christ to attend to God's purposes and to the interests of others, and not only to their own interests.

At the same time, elements of Jesus' teaching, whether by word or example, indicate more specific purposes and directions in action. These, too, accord with appropriate dispositions as well as the dominant devotion to God. As we noted earlier, Karl Barth explores a number of teachings having to do with human possessions, service in discipleship, the use of force, and so forth. For Barth, these teachings are prominent lines of Jesus' commanding that instruct Christians and lend direction to their actions.[10] Thus, for Christians, whether and, if so, how to use force against others is a perennial issue. On the face of it, at least, the use of force against creatures that God creates and sustains poses a troubling question, and the burden of proof is upon those who would employ violent or coercive means. More recently, Stanley Hauerwas has claimed that, in light of the story of Jesus Christ in the Gospels, care for the weak is a particular intention or purpose of human life appropriately related to God.[11] To these specifications, others also should be added, such as healing the sick and a special concern for the poor. The teachings of Jesus recommend and engender the kinds of intentions, purposes, and actions that are appropriate for Christians.

We should note also that the Christian community has often fastened upon a more general principle in Jesus' teaching as it is presented in the Gospels, the so-called "Golden Rule": "So whatever you wish that men would do to you, do so to them; for this is the law and the prophets" (Matt. 7:12). Again, "And as you wish that men would do to you, do so to them" (Luke 6:31). These statements reflect the longer tradition in which Jesus stands. They have Talmudic precedent in Hillel's negative summary of the law: "Do not do to your fellow what you hate to have done to you."[12] Augustine says that Matt. 7:12 expresses purity of heart, or "a heart in which God is being sought" rather than one's own temporal advantage.[13] Calvin regards Matt. 7:12 and Luke 6:31 as summaries of the rule of equity or fairness.[14] We might say that the "Golden Rule" operates as a principle of impartiality, which refuses exceptions to moral conduct on the basis of one's own private interests.[15] Again, this accords with the appropriate orientation of human life devoted to God; for the principle of fairness or impartiality, which requires that one look after the neighbor's interests with the same vigilance that one accords to one's own, expresses a dominant life orientation in which self-centeredness and inordinate self-concern have been broken by devotion to God and the things of God. Those who follow Jesus ought to be fair and impartial in their dealings with others, and the "Golden Rule" furnishes a clear guideline for self-examination.

In the context of the longer prophetic tradition, the commitment to fairness or impartiality fits well with special attention to the poor, the weak, and the outcast. This is part of the meaning of Amos's complaint against business people who are waiting for the holy season to end so that they may lawfully resume their fraudulent dealings: "Hear this, you who trample upon the needy, and bring the poor of the land to an end, saying 'When will the new moon be over, that we may sell grain?' " (Amos 8:4–5a). The constant temptation of those in positions of comfort and power is to define justice and apply it in ways that favor their own advantage and leave the plight of the marginal out of account. Care for the poor, the weak, and the outcast is an appropriate indicator of faithfulness to God and God's reign because it is a test of whether the inordinate self-concern and private interest of the comfortable have truly been broken by devotion to God or whether they have fixed the scales of justice.[16]

Jesus Christ also teaches the truth about history as God's government. He is the one who proclaims the kingdom of God whose time is coming and now is. The kingdom is an inherently social and political image which connects Jesus' preaching with the message of the prophets. It may be described as the *telos* of God's reign, a state of affairs in which relations among creatures will be appropriately ordered by their relations to God and to one another.[17] Much has been written about the eschatological thrust of Jesus' teaching. Here, it is sufficient to note the profound tension between the present and the impending fulfillment of God's reign that this introduces into the Christian life.[18] The kingdom has drawn near in Jesus Christ. It is both present and future. Indeed, the transvaluation precipitated by the kingdom ("So the last will be first, and the first last," Matt. 20:16) coheres with things like the purpose and intention to care for the weak and downtrodden that are already appropriate responses in God's world.

The kingdom is like a prism by whose light things appear as they truly are. The message of the kingdom is a call to repentance because fulfillment of God's reign in human lives requires that devotion to God rule human hearts and that the lesser, misguided loyalties that chronically dominate, skew, and enslave human life be ordered by this cardinal devotion. Thus, the coming kingdom is judgment because God's reign exacts a tragic price for misoriented and misdirected actions of egoism, disobedience, and inordinate self-assertion, namely, the suffering of the innocent for the sins of the guilty. So, for example, suffering for the sins of parents often falls, not on the parents themselves, but on their children. Writing during the Second World War, H. Richard Niebuhr observed that suffering for the sins of a Hitler and a Nazi party falls indiscriminately on the Finns and the French, on the children of Cologne and Coventry.[19] The vision of a new heaven and a new earth contrasts with the present order where God's will remains undone.

At the same time, the coming kingdom is also promise. It holds out the prospect of a changed world in which love of God motivates and orders dispositions and actions that attend to the good of others, and so disturbs the sinister cycle of sinful misdirection. In addition, then, to confidence in and loyalty to God, and alongside repentance and remorse, the message of the kingdom introduces hope as a basic qualification of Christian affectivity. This hope is neither wild nor fanatic, since it is anchored in a true understanding of God's order of grace as one that affords possibilities for reconciliation and renewal. Indeed, Christian hope correlates with patience, since we are called upon to hope for things that are not yet seen.[20] Nevertheless, it also expresses the tension between our present manner of living and the coming kingdom. The nearness of the kingdom precipitates a crisis because, as Jack Dean Kingsbury puts it with reference to the Gospel of Matthew, "encounter with the Kingdom means that a person must decide: will he enter the 'narrow gate' and take the 'hard way' that leads to 'life,' or will he enter the 'wide gate' and take the 'broad way' that leads to 'destruction' (7:13–14)?"[21] By his proclamation of the kingdom whose time is coming and now is, Jesus calls us to remember the way of the Lord, just as the prophets called Israel to return to its vocation as God's people.[22]

So, in words and in deed, Jesus Christ is the one who teaches the truth. He instructs us about the world as God's dominion, about the dominant devotion that orients authentic life in relation to God, and about dispositions, purposes, intentions, and actions that are appropriate to that dominant devotion. He teaches a principle of impartiality, and he instructs us in the coming judgment and promise of God's kingdom.

THE ONE WHO EMBODIES THE WAY

Yet Jesus Christ not only teaches the truth; he also embodies a way that accords with the truth. Here we affirm much of what has been meant in the tradition by Jesus' kingly activity. Christ governs the Christian life both inwardly and outwardly. He recapitulates the way of God with Israel as it was expressed through the institution of the kingship, by means of those who were anointed to rule God's people in divine sonship and service. The Greek word *archegos,* used with reference to Jesus by the writers of Acts and Hebrews, seems well suited to suggest this confluence of embodiment and governance. In the Revised Standard Version, it is translated by the word "pioneer" and evokes the image of a pathfinder. In its wider range of meaning, it signifies one who begins something and also supplies the impetus, the originator, founder, guide, captain, leader, prince, or ruler.[23]

Jesus Christ embodies a way of life that is oriented by trust in and loyalty to God as its dominant devotion. He therefore not only proclaims this loyalty and gives verbal instruction about dispositions, purposes, and intentions that accord with it; he also displays this devotion together with appropriate dispositions, purposes, intentions, and actions in his life. He expresses the dominant devotion in his obedience to God, even unto death on the cross. He displays love to neighbor as well as appropriate dispositions such as humility and appropriate purposes such as healing in his associations with the sick, the oppressed, the downtrodden, and the reviled, and by his insistence that the disciples allow the little children to come to him.[24]

What I mean to indicate here by the language of embodiment and display is something like what Edwards meant by "the temper of Jesus" expressed in his teaching, example, and, above all, in "his last sufferings." Edwards lists virtues like humility, meekness, love, forgiveness, and mercy.[25] Augustine is tireless in his insistence that the mediator displays the humility of God and, as we have seen, Calvin also has high regard for this virtue in contrast to pride and arrogance.[26] Others might be mentioned. Precise lists of virtues, dispositions, attitudes, and intentions that contribute to a certain temper are notoriously difficult to devise. My point here, however, is only that, by his example of certain kinds of action in the service of loyalty to God, Jesus Christ marks off a path or a way that governs the Christian life both inwardly and outwardly. In this, he is related to Christians as leader to followers, pathfinder to travelers.

Like Jesus' teachings, this way functions both imperatively and persuasively. Christians ought to lead lives in alignment with Christ's pattern. On the other hand, people follow him only when they share his dominant loyalty or devotion to God. And, when they do, then they also find a certain excellence or attractiveness in Christ's pattern of allegiance, action, and endurance. This too is part of what helps to engender Christ-likeness in them.

Calvin describes this way as one of self-denial, and this appears to indicate an attitude or orientation engendered by right confidence in and loyalty to God rather than a rational moral principle. Because of this, one of his prime metaphors for discipleship is service; because we are not our own and because we are devoted to God, we should subordinate our self-concern to our loyalty to God and "follow the leading of the Lord alone." Moreover, self-denial and the dispositions of humility, earnestness, and so forth that accord with it also give us "the right attitude toward our fellow men," one that is ready to attend with true reverence to others who also stand in relation to God. So self-denial is not a moral principle but an expression of that devotion to God in light of which Christians are to order their lives both inwardly and outwardly. It is an attitude, basic orientation, or stance in accordance with which one understands the significance of moral principles such as generosity and beneficence.[27] Edwards appears to have a similar point in mind when he identifies true virtue as love of God and contrasts the benevolence to "being in general" that it engenders with inordinate self-love or concern for one's own private interest.[28] Benevolence to "being in general" is not a moral principle such as justice or truth-telling. It does not prescribe specific actions. Rather, it characterizes an overall attitude in terms of which the importance of principles of justice and truth-telling are understood.

Indeed, self-denial is an unavoidable part of ordinary life because human identity is formed in the service of a cause. Self-denial is the posture of someone who is devoted to a cause, and is therefore willing to qualify or even sacrifice other interests and desires when loyalty to the cherished cause should require it.[29] As Charles Swezey has written,

> This is true of all life. Parents gain identity as parents to the extent that family is served. Patriots gain identity as patriots to the extent that country is served. Physicians gain identity as physicians to the extent that health is served. In each instance, such loyalty is costly to other interests.[30]

In a sense, devotion to a cherished cause redirects or rebalances the person. It engenders a particular orientation, stance, or direction in light of which one may order or prioritize various needs, wants, and desires.

This is one way to interpret Mark 8:34*b*–36 and its parallels. What is at stake here—in denying oneself, in taking up one's cross, in following Jesus, and in losing one's life in order to find it—is not a rational moral principle, but an abiding and orienting loyalty. One gains one's life orientation, movement, and identity from loyalty to a cause. As Richard R. Niebuhr points out, in our attempts to understand people, "their acts of creativity and self-destruction remain obscure to us until we grasp the passion that tempers their hearts and the cause or occasion that has brought the passion to birth in them."[31] The question of life is always whether one's dominant cause is truly worthy of allegiance, of becoming the crimson thread from which one spins one's identity. And Jesus' teaching and example constantly pose this question precisely because his own personal balance so transparently hinges upon radical devotion to God.

The cause to which Jesus is loyal and to which he calls others is the power that governs all things, or what Edwards called "being in general." Therefore, this devotion engenders an affective balance and identity that is radically opposed to inordinate self-concern. It engenders an attitude that is ready to attend to all others, and it coheres with dispositions such as humility and a readiness to forgive those whose actions have injured one's own private interests.

Yet for Christians Jesus Christ does not just embody a way of life that commends and engenders certain attitudes, dispositions, purposes, intentions, and actions. He does not just embody a passion or devotion capable of answering the question of identity. He also embodies a way that coheres and is congruent with God's dominion. The way that Jesus embodies truthfully answers the question of how we are to respond to the powers that bear down upon us in our history. As followers of Jesus who share his loyalty and cause, we are to respond to these powers as elements that exist within the realm of grace and are governed by the reign of God whose *telos* is the kingdom of judgment and promise. We are called to respond to these powers as elements that exist under God's dominion. The one who walks in the way is therefore called to consent to these powers as agencies that express God's purposes. He or she is called to give thanks for them where they sustain the delicate fabric of interdependent relations among creatures, to suffer them where they deliver judgment upon our sins, and to celebrate them when they afford possibilities for reconciliation and renewal. This, however, does not mean that one is called passively to endure or actively to abet their every arrangement, influence, or action. The Christian life is not a counsel of despairing acquiescence. To be sure, people are dependent creatures who must learn to accept their true limitations. Manipulation in any corner of creation or arena of life risks unintended and uncontrolled consequences, as is apparent from our growing experience with the delicate fabric of interdependent social, cultural, and ecological relations. Yet one who is aware of creaturely limitations may give thanks for a power that sustains and also endeavor to enhance it. One may celebrate a power that reconciles or renews and also pursue the possibilities that it presents. So also one may suffer a power as judgment and yet repent of one's sins and work to transform or contain that power, its influences, and their tragic results.

A way of life that fits with God's reign and realm of grace is one that is in alignment with an order that exacts a tragic price for actions of inordinate self-assertion as well as for slothful or quietistic acquiescence to the inordinate assertions of others. It need not promise people success in all their efforts to bring about good in order to supply those efforts with motivation as well as a vision that informs and directs them. There is a time to celebrate promise, but also to pursue the hopes that promise holds forth. There is a time to suffer judgment and to repent, but also to try to mitigate or avoid coming judgment and its tragedies.

Somewhat like the figure of the king in ancient Israel, Jesus Christ is the anointed one *par excellence*. He stands in a relationship of loyal sonship to God the Father and he rules as God's heir. This sonship involves him in a "double movement—with men toward God, with God toward men; from the world to the Other, from the Other to the world."[32] As the one who embodies the way, Jesus points away from the many powers and values of the world toward the One who alone is good and powerful; again, by his love, justice, hope, obedience, faithfulness, and humility he points back to the world and mediates God's purposes to us. He marks off the way of self-denial in the service of God as ultimate cause, and he shows us how to walk by his example of appropriate dispositions, purposes, intentions, and actions. He suggests to us a distinct identity or vocation, and in this sense, he guides or governs the Christian life.

Does this mean that Jesus bears a distinctive politics? Certainly not in the more usual or conventional sense of favoring a specific institutional variety of government, say a republican or parliamentary form. Yet, if by "politics" one means, more loosely, a form, orientation, or quality of social life, then the answer is considerably more positive. One cannot set loyalty to God above all other loyalties, appeal to the kingdom as judgment and as promise, call self-centered and misdirected people to repentance, restrain the use of force, insist upon fairness or impartiality, care for the poor, engender and require attentiveness to the needs and interests of others, and still approach people as fundamentally alien or strange in terms of one's lesser loyalties to nation, class, or race.

THE ONE WHO EMPOWERS THE LIFE

For those who follow Jesus, the devotion to God that orders lesser loyalties to family, nation, or race, and that accords with dispositions such as humility, purposes such as reconciliation, and actions such as caring for the weak, is the only way into the kingdom of God or the *telos* of God's reign. The issue of redemption therefore becomes the question of how sinful people, who are curved in upon themselves and in bondage to self-concern, who are chronically confused in their loyalties, misoriented in their lives, and misdirected in their actions, can be gripped by that devotion to the supreme cause and reality that governs all things.

There are many ways in which inordinate self-concern, misorientation, and misdirection may be broken. The half-gods that capture our lesser loyalties may fail. This is what H. Richard Niebuhr once called "the twilight of the gods."[33] The nationalist may suffer the decay of the nation. The executive may suffer corporate and financial defeat. One's family may be irreparably hurt or disrupted.

Occasions such as these may impress one with the fact that none of these lesser gods is sufficient to invest life with meaning, that none of them is truly worthy of ultimate allegiance. But, for Christians, these catastrophic failures or twilights of the false gods and idols are always accompanied by Jesus Christ, the one who imparts the power of God that enables sinners to turn toward what is true, to walk in the way, and to lead lives in alignment with his own. To say this is to affirm the sacrificial dimension of Christ's work that often has been designated in the tradition as his priestly activity. Jesus Christ recapitulates God's way with Israel as it is expressed through the cultic priesthood. He is the minister of a new holiness who, by his sacrifice on the cross, mediates between God and fallen humanity. He is the power of God. In Paul's words, "For the word of the cross is folly to those who are perishing, but to us who are being saved it is the power of God" (1 Cor. 1:18). Again: "For I am not ashamed of the gospel: it is the power of God for salvation to every one who has faith, to the Jew first and also to the Greek" (Rom. 1:16).

Jesus Christ is the one who communicates the life because he is the one who imparts the power of God that turns people from sin and sets them in the way to God's kingdom. This power is the power to change hearts, to engender confidence in and loyalty to God as a dominant, orienting devotion. So, for example, Augustine describes God's re-creation of people as the fashioning of a new heart, and he attributes "the enlargement of your hearts" to the operation of God's grace.[34] Edwards speaks of regeneration as a work of God's Spirit that provides people with a new spiritual sense attended by a "new holy disposition of heart." It is this that enables the saint to be motivated by "the divine excellency of God, and of Jesus Christ" rather than by private interest.[35]

What both Augustine and Edwards have in mind is the power that enables repentance and new life, or the power of transformation. Christians confess that if this power had not come to them, they should all have gone astray. For as people whose hearts are constricted and curved in upon ourselves and our private goods, we haven't the hearts to follow the way. And, since our actions reflect and proceed from our orienting devotions or affections, we cannot by our own actions work the needed alteration in ourselves. As the one who imparts the power of God, Jesus Christ does what is impossible for us. He works a revolution in our hearts that turns us toward God and others. Again, this appears to be what Calvin has in mind when he says that the mediator "would have come to us in vain if he had not been furnished with this power," the power of the Holy Spirit "by which we come to enjoy Christ and all his benefits." [36]

This power is not, as the New Testament writers clearly understood, the power of nations and empires, or of princes and kings. It is rather a power made perfect in weakness, the power of the cross. Here, we may observe with Reinhold Niebuhr that the Christ who comes is not the messiah who was expected. [37] We confront a truly startling claim. The power that governs and reigns over all things is perfected in tragic suffering rather than oppressive might. Jesus' crucifixion is the great occasion of innocent suffering unto death that hangs over all the many occasions of innocent suffering that continue to be the wages of sin in our history. This is the great occasion that brings a new passion to birth in people, that introduces devotion to the ultimate cause into our history as the dominant loyalty that orients authentic human life.

We can say more about this. The innocent one who was crucified at Calvary suffered the consequences of the sins of others. This is the great parable or analogy, the discerning lens through which Christians look at the world. When Christians look through that lens, then they discern the many other Calvaries both great and small that clutter the horizons of our world. They see the innocent suffering still for the sins of the guilty—for our sins—on many an obscure hill. And in this suffering they see the cross. [38]

Something like this has often been expressed in Christian art and literature. Josiah Royce explains it by referring to Johann Sebastian Bach's *St. Matthew's Passion*. At the last supper,

> Christ has just said: "One of you shall betray me." "And they all begin to say . . . 'Is it I? Is it I? Is it I?' " And then there begins . . . the chorus of "the Believers"; " 'Tis I, *My* sins betray thee, who died to make me whole."

The effect is that "an old story of the past retold" becomes the listener's own. The believer "sees the betrayal, the divine tragedy and the triumph. . . . In this vision all flows and changes and passes from the sorrows of a whole world to the hope of reconciliation." [39]

The power of this great occasion is for Christians the power to bring about God's kingdom. To all but the hardest of hearts, it is the power that is able to work a change of heart, the power to make people turn from the way of inordinate self-concern toward the way, the truth, and the life marked off by Jesus Christ. It is the power that moves people to repent of their sins because it punctuates and underscores and will not let them turn their gaze from the sight of sin's tragic consequences, namely, the suffering of God's own Son. "Out of such despair contrition is born; and of contrition faith is conceived; and in that faith there is 'newness of life,' which is to say 'power.' "[40] This power made perfect in weakness is one that often inhabits the underside of history, but it persists as an undying protest against the insatiable desires of every oppressive agent. It is, quite simply, the power to change hearts that enables people to follow the one who was crucified and despised. And—this is the crucial point—through the life, death, and resurrection of Jesus Christ, Christians have been led to the conviction that this is the perfected expression of divine power, the great clue to the character of the divine reality that orders and governs all things.

By now it must be apparent that my thematization of the particularity of Jesus Christ has consequences for the way in which atonement may be understood. To say not only that Jesus Christ once suffered the consequences of the sins of others, but also that he suffered for our sins, entails, in my view, at least three additional observations.

First, Jesus' crucifixion was an outcome of his ministry in the sense that his crucifixion was the response of certain people and powers to his message of the kingdom and his representation of a way of life oriented by devotion to God and love of neighbor.[41] Here, as in the history of Israel, inordinate and misdirected loyalties to the half-gods come into conflict with loyalty to the one universal cause. It is often debated whether the crucifixion of Jesus represents a Roman misinterpretation of his ministry, since crucifixion was a punishment meted out to political threats. The answer, I suspect, is both yes and no. Yes, because Jesus' ministry was not based in a loyalty to a specific government, form of government, or zealot revolution. No, because his loyalty to God and God's kingdom together with its attendant dispositions, intentions, and directions in action did indeed imply a politics or quality of social life at odds with the prevailing politics of the

established authorities. Moreover, as the Gospel portraits of Gethsemane try to show, Jesus is aware of conflict between various mundane
powers and the requirements of his ministry, and there is a connection
between his consent to his fate and his loyalty to God and God's reign.
It therefore makes sense to say that his death is of a piece with his life
and ministry.

Second, sinful actions are not simply individualistic or isolated
expressions of inner dispositions but are, in fact, socially intercon-
nected. There is such a thing as what Friedrich Schleiermacher once
called the corporate aspect or dimension of sin, or what Walter Rauschenbusch was suggesting when he referred to a "solidaristic conception of sin."[42] Sin's misdirection or constriction of the heart—its
loyalties, attitudes, purposes, intentions, and so on—has a personal
basis in the complex and even conflicting aspects of human emotional
constitution. Individuals chronically prioritize and order elements of
their emotional constitutions in inappropriate, misdirected, disobedient, and destructive ways. This misdirection or constriction becomes
embodied in particular actions and these actions shape the social ethos,
institutions, and customary patterns of interaction in our history.
These structures, in turn, work upon the emotional or affective constitutions of people. By social appropriation, then, manners of living
that engender and elicit misoriented affections are transmitted to others.[43] It is, therefore, not too much to say, with Schleiermacher, that
sin is "in each the work of all and in all the work of each."[44] Indeed,
it makes more sense to speak of an objective power of sin at work in
the world, or even of a kingdom of sin or evil, than at first glance it
might appear.

Third, like Jesus Christ, the innocent continue to suffer the consequences of the sins of the guilty. Here and now, they continue to
suffer the consequences of our sins. Therefore, the suffering of Jesus
on the cross is more than a parable or an analogy. It is a demonstration
of the very order of reality, the disclosure of a fundamental pattern
in our moral experience.[45]

If these conditions can be met, then the way is clear to draw the
following conclusion. Out of loyalty to God and love of neighbor,
Jesus Christ endured his last sufferings at the hands of sinners. Yet his
crucifixion was at the hands not only of the particular people who put

him to death, but also "at the hands of" the power of sin in our history that continues to infect our own hearts. Bach is therefore quite correct in his Passion music to put the words, "'Tis I, *My* sins betray thee" into the recurrent chorale of the chorus of "the Believers."

Because it hangs over all other occasions of innocent suffering in our history, the great occasion of Christ's crucifixion changes the meaning of our sin and of the tragic suffering that it causes. Our sins and the innocent sufferings they cause now become occasions for repentance and a change of heart. Indeed, when we view the corporate kingdom of sin and its continuous dominion through the ages and generations, then it is not too much to say that the cross has turned sin's power against itself. Sin's kingdom is now a house divided. The very occasions that were to build up and contribute to sin's solidaristic dominion have now been transformed. We may therefore speak of Christ's victory over the kingdom of sin, a victory that has turned the very fact of sin and its infectious power toward repentance and reconciliation. This, of course, does not mean that sin has ceased to exist, but it does mean that its power and dominion have been dealt a crippling blow.

This theme may be developed further. Jesus is the one who remains unconquered by the forces of sin and destruction in human life. He is unconquered in his heart by pride, or the way of aggression, and by sloth, or the way of withdrawal, because in his heart he remains loyal to God and to others. This too is a way of expressing the victory of the cross. Jesus remains faithful to the community between God and creation precisely because he remains unconquered by sin's power and its kingdom, by the forces that disrupt the community among God and creatures. As Gustaf Wingren puts it, "Jesus' life can be said to constitute the reconquest of the created order, the halting of destruction." Or again, "the prayer for the soldier and the promise to the malefactor on the side-cross are audible expressions of a deeper victory which cannot be heard and is not seen."[46] The innocent one who suffers at the hands of the power of sin in our history is not driven to ask that his suffering be avenged; neither does he withdraw into stoical detachment. Instead, by asking that his executioners be forgiven and that the malefactor receive new life, he turns the tragedy of his own crucifixion into the lasting occasion for repentance that hangs over all other occasions of innocent suffering.

This is atonement, the occasion of suffering endurance in which the kingdom of God, or the *telos* of God's reign, has drawn near. It is the occasion that imparts the power to change human hearts and the work that has changed the objective situation of humanity in God's world. It does not eliminate the tragedy of sin; neither does it allow us to forget sin's many inroads. But it does enable us, as it once enabled Augustine in his *Confessions,* to bring sin's betrayals and tragic consequences to light and to find new meaning in them. Atonement does not make either sin or tragedy good. But it does furnish new possibilities. Sin and the consequential suffering of the innocent now comprise the moving, costly, and tragic occasion for the possibility of renewal and new life. The redemptive power of Christ's suffering lends transformative force to other occasions of unearned suffering.[47] This, finally, is the "awe full" and also the awful mystery of the cross. To those who are perishing it is the darkest folly, but to those who are being saved it is the power of God made perfect in weakness. We may articulate this mystery, although most often theologians do so less poignantly than do artists and musicians; but we cannot dispel the mystery or go beyond it.

This outline of the atonement does not repeat any single articulation of that doctrine in classic Christian tradition, although it retrieves important elements or aspects from a number of traditional statements. Christ's sacrifice removes sin's solidaristic penalty. Although I have not duplicated Anselm's emphasis on the penal satisfaction of divine honor, this claim underscores the suffering of the innocent one for our sins.[48] Christ's work awakens repentance in the hearts of others. Like Abelard, I have tried to account for a more personal bond of affection between Jesus Christ and ourselves, although I have also tried to articulate a more objective connection in the order of God's world.[49] The claim that Jesus Christ remains unconquered by the power of sin is an attempt to retrieve something like Martin Luther's focus on "Christ's work as a conflict and triumph," or the conquest of sin and the devil through Christ the victor.[50] Particularly at this point, my formulation makes use of the corporate or solidaristic notion of sin developed by leading liberal theologians during the nineteenth and twentieth centuries. My interpretation, with its emphasis on the continuing suffering of the innocent for the sins of the guilty, like H. Richard Niebuhr's position in his articles about the Second World War, would not be possible without Horace Bushnell's work on *The Vicarious Sacrifice*. The idea that others participate in the order of sacrifice and suffering patience that Christ fulfills is Bushnell's.[51] The claim that Christ's crucifixion alters the meaning of sin and its tragic consequences in our history owes much to this same American theologian, who delivered his manuscript on Christ's work to the publisher as the nation mourned Lincoln's death. Bushnell "dared to think" that the Civil War "could be good in some way akin to the way in which Good Friday was good."[52]

Finally, my understanding of atonement affirms that the cross is a basic criterion for truly Christian life and theology. The issue here is partly one of discernment, and in this context Luther's thesis cannot be repeated too often. "The 'theologian of glory' calls the bad good and the good bad. The 'theologian of the cross' says what a thing is."[53] Indeed, one may say that it is possible to be a Christ to the neighbor only when I begin to see Christ in my neighbor. "For I was hungry and you gave me food, I was thirsty and you gave me drink, I was a stranger and you welcomed me, I was sick and you visited me, I was in prison and you came to me" (Matt. 25:35–36).[54] Gustavo Gutiérrez is surely correct in connection with this passage to note that "it is not enough to say that love of God is inseparable from the love of one's neighbor. It must be added love for God is unavoidably expressed through love of one's neighbor."[55] Calvin is understandably concerned that this passage not be read as an endorsement of works righteousness, and he also shows a tendency inappropriately to limit those in need to the community of the faithful. Nevertheless, the strong connection between this passage and Jesus' prophetic concern for the poor and those in need shines through also in his exposition:

> Christ is either neglected or given care in the person of those who need our assistance. As often as we are reluctant to help the poor let the sight of the Son of God come before our eyes, for to deny him anything is sacrilege of the deepest order.[56]

Jesus Christ empowers new life. His cross hangs over all other occasions of innocent suffering, and so, by his costly sacrifice, he enables sinners to repent and walk in the way. He remains unconquered by sin's death-dealing power and so wins the victory over sin's solidaristic dominion. Therefore, the crucified one is the power of God made perfect in weakness.

HIS CONTINUING PRESENCE

As the one who teaches the truth, embodies the way, and empowers the life, Jesus Christ constitutes what Joseph Sittler has called "the engendering deed."[57] This deed has a particular affective balance; it has a specifiable pattern, shape, or morphology that informs our vision of God and of human life in appropriate relation to God. Jesus' resurrection attests to the validity of this deed, to this truth about God's dominion, to this way into God's kingdom, and to this life in God's power. Indeed, if the early communities had not been persuaded that Jesus Christ was the risen Lord and living presence in their experience, then the specific contours of the way, the truth, and the life in him would have disappeared from our history. The resurrection is a symbol held by Christians for nearly twenty centuries. It lifts up, holds forth, and maintains the continuing presence of God's way with humanity in Jesus Christ. The resurrection enables Christians to look back upon this deed and see it in its proper light. For it is the reality of Jesus Christ as continuing presence that enables the Gospel writers as well as those who have come after them to talk about the way, the truth, and the life in him. Thus, by his continuing presence, Jesus Christ becomes the teacher who continues to instruct, the leader who continues to guide, the power who continues to empower. He becomes the great occasion that hangs over all other occasions in our history, the power of reconciliation and renewal that is still with us, the one who shares his victory with others in a widening circle. For the Christian community, Jesus' resurrection signifies the vindication of the crucified one as God's own Son, God's "yes" to the way, the truth, and the life embodied in the man from Nazareth.

I am not insensitive to the fact that this interpretation yields few hard and fast rules for the preacher at Easter. Perhaps this is as it should be:

> Only poets can do justice to the Christmas and Easter stories and
> there are not many poets in the pulpit. It is better therefore to be
> satisfied with the symbolic presentation of the poetry in hymn,
> anthem, and liturgy. The sermons which interpret these stories
> usually make a rational defense of their historic validity or they
> qualify them rationally to make them acceptable to the intel-
> lect. . . . I suppose it is necessary and inevitable that the poetry
> of religion should be expressed in rational terms but something
> is always lost in the rationalization.[58]

What does seem most appropriate at Easter is for the Christian community to celebrate in Christ God's ultimate triumph over evil, victory
over sin, and sovereignty over death.

The precise nature of Jesus' resurrection is a controversial topic
partly because the New Testament itself presents no single consistent
portrait or theory. Some passages appear to assume the raising of Jesus'
physical body. Others imply something considerably less tangible.
One thing on which there is wide agreement in the New Testament,
however, is that early Christians had experiences of the continuing
presence of Jesus Christ after his crucifixion.

Karl Barth claims that the resurrection is physical and that the
disciples had "an objective" encounter with the risen Jesus.[59] Others,
like Emil Brunner, speak of an event involving a self or center of the
personality that is not at all material.[60] However, extended dogmatic
discussions of this question almost always miss the forest for the trees.
They do not really come to terms with the larger implication of the
fact that seemingly contradictory portraits of the risen Lord in his
appearances were allowed to stand side by side in the New Testament.
Why should the early communities have been comfortable with this?
The answer, I suspect, is that they were considerably less concerned
about the physical or nonphysical nature of the resurrection "event"
than are many of our contemporaries. For the early Christian communities, this was not where the main significance of the statement
"He is risen" lay. The primary importance of that confession was the
reality of Jesus Christ as the risen Lord of their continuing experience.[61]

This conclusion accords also with the rather minimal and Bult-
mannian interpretation of Jesus' resurrection offered by Willi Marxsen.
"The declaration that Jesus has risen came to be made" as "an inference
derived from personal faith." For Marxsen, the words "Jesus is risen"

essentially mean that "the cause of Jesus continues; or in the words of the hymn, 'still he comes today.' "[62] Again, Peter Hodgson, who accepts the basic outline of Marxsen's interpretation, says that the resurrection "is an inference from a present experience to a past occasion for this experience." It "is an *historic* event in its *present* modality, not as an historically observable past event."[63] To these statements, we may add that still he comes today as the one who teaches the truth, embodies the way, and empowers the life.

CONCLUSION

I believe that the thematization of the symbolic pattern of Jesus Christ which I have presented here has a number of virtues. It is congruent with what we know about the Jesus of history and his manner of life. It neglects neither Jesus' teaching and example in favor of his sacrifice, nor his sacrifice in favor of his teaching and example. Although it is necessarily selective in its choice of fundamental metaphors and images, it nevertheless attempts to take seriously a wide cross-section of New Testament literature. It accounts for the impact of Jesus Christ in our history on the characters of human subjects, but anchors that subjective influence in an objective victory over the power of sin in the historic epic of Christ's life, ministry, sacrifice, and resurrection, and in the truth about God's dominion in the world. Like the twofold and threefold patterns present in the theological tradition, my thematization exhibits a double character or direction that parallels the centrality of Jesus Christ secured by the early councils. Jesus Christ is understood as authentic humanity appropriately directed toward God. He is acknowledged also as the power of God who redirects people who have lost their true relation to God. In him humanity is directed toward God and God comes to humanity.

Nothing less than this seems entailed by Luke 2:11, "for to you is born this day in the city of David a Savior." Jesus Christ is the prophet who proclaims God's kingdom and teaches the truth. He is the king who governs true life and protects the creation from wayward destruction. He is the perfect sacrifice, the deliverer who saves his people from their sins by liberating them from bondage to the power of sin.

5

The Mediator

Whom could I find to reconcile me to you? Ought I to have sought the help of the angels?

—Augustine, *Confessions*

Jesus Christ is central for our knowledge of God and of ourselves. The New Testament employs a variety of images and symbols to convey this. Jesus Christ is God's son born of a virgin, he is the anointed one, the wisdom of God, the true light that shines in darkness, and so forth. The truth that Jesus Christ is decisive for our apprehensions of God and human life is a supreme claim of the Christian religion; why it should be true is a supreme wonderment.

As we have seen, the Chalcedonian Definition may be interpreted as a classic document that further develops and secures this claim against a number of challenges in the Hellenistic world. Just because it responds to these challenges, Chalcedon is considerably more exact about the centrality of Jesus Christ than is the more extensive and varied literature of the New Testament. If one asks, "In what sense is Jesus Christ central?" Chalcedon answers, "In the sense that he is decisive for both our apprehension of God and our apprehension of human life in appropriate relation to God; although the reality of God is not collapsed into authentic humanity or vice versa, neither is knowledge of Jesus Christ knowledge of some third reality." Chalcedon therefore indicates how we may conceive of the claim that here the final and most profound mystery of life is focused in a particular individual; Jesus Christ is actually God and actually man, two natures in one person, united hypostatically.

Like many other modern theologians, I find this doctrine flawed as a substantive specification of the centrality of Jesus Christ, and I see little point in continually sharpening or refining its terms on the assumption that we may somehow arrive upon a satisfactory univocal statement. The mystery is too profound to be captured in a literal phrase or concept. At Chalcedon, poetry was transmuted into dogma, but into a kind of fractured or symbolic dogma that points beyond itself, a dogma that, by its novel use of the terms of Hellenistic metaphysics, has forever cheated the philosophers out of a tidy explanation. If, however, Chalcedon is understood as a symbolic statement that further develops and secures the centrality of Jesus Christ in its particular time and place, then the way is clear to regard it as the dogmatic, historically conditioned form in which the Hellenistic church articulated an enduring insight. My intention in this chapter, then, is to offer an alternative and contemporary symbolization of the centrality of Jesus Christ, one that remains informed by the lasting truth secured by Chalcedon, though it does not repeat Chalcedon's celebrated definition.[1]

THE SUPREME MEDIATION OF THE REALITY OF GOD

If we no longer understand the centrality of Jesus Christ with the aid of a metaphysical portrait of two natures in one hypostasis, with the aid of what symbol shall we now understand it? Sometimes, while trying to understand the complexities of a difficult problem, one comes across a short statement that sheds light on the whole. For me, D. M. Baillie has offered such a statement about the centrality of Jesus Christ. It appears in the fifth chapter of his famous book *God Was in Christ*. We turn to Baillie's essential argument.

There is a paradox at the heart of the Christian life whose "essence lies in the conviction which a Christian man possesses, that every good thing in him, every good thing he does, is somehow not wrought by himself but by God."[2] There is a human side to good actions, but the grace of God is prior. Now this paradox, says Baillie, is a clue to the mystery of Jesus Christ. He is the one who is perfectly obedient to God, whose every action is good. In light of the paradox of grace, this is as much as to say that he is human and that he is perfectly receptive to God's grace:

> Was Jesus divine because He lived a perfect life, or was He able
> to live a perfect life because He was divine? . . . If our whole line
> of thought has been correct, this question does not present us
> with a genuine dilemma. It must, of course, be true that His
> choices were genuinely human choices, and that in a sense every-
> thing depended upon them. . . . And yet as soon as we have said
> that, we must inevitably turn round and say something apparently
> opposite, remembering that in the last analysis such human choice
> is never prevenient or even co-operative, but wholly dependent
> on the divine providence. We must say that in the perfect life of
> Him who was "*always* doing the things that are pleasing to God,"
> this divine prevenience was nothing short of incarnation.[3]

Baillie's line of thought is suggestive because it indicates a promising alternative to Chalcedon's two-natures doctrine as an expression
of the centrality of Jesus Christ. From my perspective, the difficulty
with Baillie's proposal is that it is focused almost entirely on obedient
will in action and therefore precludes much of what I have said about
the importance of dispositions, affections, and intentions for an adequate understanding of what Jesus Christ says, does, and endures. But
what if one employs a different anthropology? What if one gives priority to the heart over the will? What sort of symbolic statement of the
centrality of Jesus Christ emerges then?

The paradox of grace remains that the person of faith ascribes
the good that is in him or her to God. This is because the good that
one does flows from one's heart, yet we haven't the strength to change
or reorient our hearts. Our words and deeds are expressive of our
hearts, or of our dominant devotions and their attendant affections,
yet the orientations of our hearts are not self-chosen but result from
influences that impinge upon us. The objects we love have much to
do with who we are, yet our loves are not self-made. They befall us.

We often love our families, although as any son, daughter, or
parent knows, we rarely choose them. The patriot is loyal to the nation
and its cause. He or she therefore chooses to perform actions that
faithfully express that loyalty. But the emergence of that devotion is
largely the result of social influences (e.g., family, local community,
and national life), which are beyond his or her choosing. This is true
also of one's devotion to God. When one's actions flow from confidence in and loyalty to God, then we may say with Augustine, "It is
not of him that willeth . . . but of God that showeth mercy—the

preparation of the heart is from the Lord."[4] The critical question of life is just as Augustine claimed: What is it that one loves?

Now, this emendation of Baillie's proposal moves not only in the direction of Augustine, but also toward Jonathan Edwards's statement that "true religion, in great part, consists in holy affections."[5] It agrees with John Calvin's conviction that assent to God and God's goodness "is more of the heart than of the brain, and more of the disposition than of the understanding."[6] The paradox of grace parallels what is sometimes called the bondage of the will. Grace works upon and renews the heart. The heart, in turn, orients our wills and directs our actions so that we may freely pursue the good. But we cannot choose or manipulate the dominant orientations of our hearts. Richard R. Niebuhr makes this point when he notes the "givenness or fatality of affection," and observes the inadequacies of conceptions of faith as a virtue of reasoning or of will. "A true affection lies at such a depth in personal existence that it is inaccessible to volition. So much is clear from the fact that it is affection that endows the will with its specific tone and energy."[7]

When we turn to Jesus Christ, what we find is a person whose heart is radically gripped by confidence in and loyalty to God. This dominant devotion orients his attitudes, dispositions, purposes, intentions, and actions. It is the affection that endows his will with a specific tone and energy, and is displayed in the whole of his life and ministry, even unto death on a cross. By his words, deeds, and endurance we discern that Jesus' heart remains unconquered by that power of sin that poisons human hearts with inordinate constriction, egoism, pride, misdirection, and misorientation.

There is nothing inhuman about this. Like us, Jesus is one whose life is oriented by a dominant devotion. Like us, he is one whose choices and actions are directed by the dominant orientation of his heart. Like us, he does not choose or fabricate his dominant loyalty on his own. His dominant devotion and the orientation in life that it supports are not, in this fundamental sense, self-chosen or self-willed. Rather, the emergence of this dominant orientation in him must be understood as his response to influences upon him in nature and in history, to the powers bearing down upon him.

We might speak of these powers and influences in a variety of ways. From a biological perspective, powers and influences, genetic and otherwise, converge to fund his emotional constitution as a human being. From a psychological perspective, his dominant orientation may reflect unconscious influences rooted in experiences of early childhood. From a historical and sociological perspective, powers and influences in his Jewish heritage and social environment are arranged so as to develop or draw out his biologically given and psychologically formed constitution in particular ways and directions. We need not choose between the forces of "nature" and "nurture" in the formation of the man Jesus any more than we must in ourselves.[8]

In a theological perspective, however, the powers and influences of both nature and nurture are construed as elements within God's dominion. They are ultimately connected with the divine providence. Therefore, it makes sense to say that Jesus' orientation is the work of God's grace. Indeed, here we may cite passages from Augustine that are also quoted by Baillie:

> The Savior, the Man Christ Jesus, is himself the brightest illustration of predestination and grace. . . . Every man, from the commencement of his faith, becomes a Christian by the same grace by which *that* man from His formation becomes Christ.[9]

Rather than symbolize the centrality of Jesus Christ by two natures united in one hypostasis, then, one may depict the man Jesus as the brightest illustration of grace, or of God's affecting and dynamic power and presence. In the words of Richard R. Niebuhr, Jesus Christ is "a God-shaped man."[10] He remains faithfully responsive to God. Indeed, this is the fundamental thread that connects him with the project of our own lives, for the God to which he faithfully responds is the same ultimate reality who stands in relation to us, whether we acknowledge God or not. This is the final power in which we live and move and have our being, "the common third of past and present experience" in addition to ourselves and our creaturely companions.[11]

Precisely because he is the brightest illustration of grace or a "God-shaped man," Jesus Christ is for Christian piety the supreme mediation of the reality of God. God is experienced in and through the man Jesus. Essentially, this statement integrates christology with the wider doctrine of revelation. For the Christian community, knowledge and experience of God under the conditions of space and time are always at the same time knowledge and experience of something else. The reality of God is apprehended in and through the exodus, but the exodus is not God. The reality of God is known in and through the exile and the pronouncements of Israel's prophets, although neither the exile nor the words of the prophets are God. Like the exodus of the Israelites from Egypt, Moses at Sinai, the exile, or Isaiah in the temple, Jesus Christ is a mundane medium of revelation in and through which God is present. Unlike other media, however, Jesus is for Christians the supreme mediation of God. He differs from other media in that the whole of his life, ministry, death, and resurrection "belongs to the divine disclosure and, as the final and normative revelation, he is the *full presence* of God, an embodiment that does not admit of degree."[12] Even here, however, there can be no simple equation of the mundane medium with the reality of God itself, as Chalcedon's doctrine of the two natures makes clear. It will not do to say only that Jesus Christ is truly God. We must at the same time say that he is truly man, and take care neither to collapse nor confuse these two affirmations. Jesus Christ is a man fitted to the dynamic reality of God; he is the brightest illustration of grace. This is what makes him the supreme mediation of divine reality or the revelation of the full presence of God. This is what gives his life, ministry, death, and resurrection their distinctive balance, shape, or pattern, and this is why Jesus Christ as a pattern or symbolic form in-forms our vision of God.

THE VISION OF GOD

In the epic of Jesus' life, ministry, death, and resurrection, the mystery of the divine power that bears nature and history is clarified and, with that clarification, life is given true meaning. In Jesus Christ, God is characterized by a particular skein of relational dynamism. The ultimate power in whom we live and move is seen to be the Creator, Sustainer, Judge, and Redeemer who always already stands in relation to all; appropriately responsive creaturely existence is seen to be fitted to that morphology. Wherever one turns, the universal power and presence is there, directing creatures toward their appropriate relations to God and to one another. In short, God is for the kingdom of God.

Something like this was given metaphysical expression in much medieval theology by the pattern of *exitus et reditus*. All things proceed from and have their being in God, and all things are returned to God. God orders all things in nature and history, and God directs all things back to God. Therefore, God is for all things in their appropriate relations to God and to one another. A similar vision comes to expression in the more distinctively Protestant metaphor of God's reign. God is an active power and presence who gives existence to creation, guides it, judges it, and finally restores it to its proper state in relation to God. Therefore, God is for all things in their appropriate relations to God and to one another. Either way, the prevenient and directive dynamism of God meets creation at every turn.

The symbolic form of Jesus Christ is the part that furnishes the great clue or discerning lens by which Christians apprehend or envision the whole. In Christ, the one who teaches the truth, embodies the way, and empowers the life, the divine power that bears nature and history is seen to be the dynamic Creator, Sustainer, Judge, and Redeemer who always already stands in relation to all. In Christ, people learn humility and dependence, because God is revealed to be the power that calls all things into existence, sustains them, and redeems them. In Christ, people learn repentance and remorse, because God is revealed to be the power that judges creatures in their self-centered, disordered, and misdirected relations to God and to one another. In Christ, people learn trust, confidence, gratitude, and hope, because God is revealed to be the faithful and long-suffering Creator, Sustainer, and Redeemer who continues to stand in relation to creatures and to direct them toward their appropriate relations to God and to one another despite their persistent recalcitrance. In Christ, God is seen to be for creatures in their appropriate relations to God and to one another. God is for the kingdom of God.

It is important to explore the meaning of these last two sentences more fully. I do not say, with Karl Barth, that in Christ we see that "God is for man," because that statement is both too narrow and insufficiently nuanced.[13] It is too narrow because it inappropriately abstracts God's relation to human beings from the rest of creation, and therefore does not allow a sufficiently positive connection between creation and covenant. The relational dynamism of the God who creates all things, governs all things, and reconciles all things cannot be limited to human beings. God is always already in relation to a wider whole of creation of which humanity is a distinctive part. Barth's statement is too narrow because it neglects the interdependence of the community of creatures in their common dependence upon God. God is for *all* things in their appropriate relations to God and to one another.

But Barth's statement is also insufficiently nuanced, and this would be so even if it were changed from "God is for man" to "God is for all creation." Even that expanded statement fails adequately to account for the multidimensionality of our apprehension of God in Christ as an Other who judges as well as redeems. Barth therefore fails to communicate clearly that God is for creatures only in ways that accord with God's purposes. The statement "God is for man" exchanges too much of what Barth once called God's "otherness" for what he came to call God's "humanity." God's ways are not our ways. In Jesus Christ, God is apprehended not only as Redeemer, but also as Judge. That is why it remains important to remember that fear of the Lord is the beginning of wisdom. Jesus' message of the kingdom announces judgment as well as promise. That is why, particularly in the shadow of the cross, it is important to recognize that judgment is often indiscriminate in its choice of victims and that, in God's world, the suffering of the innocent is often the tragic and terrible cost of sin. Barth's statement is insufficiently nuanced because its vindication of the good for man remains inappropriately unqualified by the profound hiddenness of God's purposes and by the continuing experience of divine judgment. In Jesus Christ, God is for human beings only in a fashion that includes the passionate experience of Gethsemane. God is not simply for human beings. God is for human beings as well as for all creatures *in their appropriate relations to God and to one another.* God is for the kingdom of God, and that is why devotion to God and God's purposes requires a true revolution in our hearts, our values, and our commitments.

THE TRINITY[14]

In and through Jesus Christ, Christians discern the dynamic unity of God's universal power as well as varied or plural aspects of God's presence in relation to all things. That is why christology is indissolubly linked with the mystery of the Trinity. The trinitarian doctrine orders both the multidimensional variety and the dynamic unity of the Christian community's distinctive experience of God.

Thus, the names "Father," "Son," and "Spirit" indicate that nothing less than the truth, the way, and the life comprise a full or complete apprehension of divine reality. Jesus Christ teaches the truth about the world as God's dominion. He points to the power at work in all things. Therefore, knowledge of the one who teaches the truth attests to the Lord of existence that Christians call "the Father." It indicates that divine reality is mediated in creative, sustaining, threatening, and promising forms as a dynamic power and presence in and through experiences of nature, history, and society. Again, Jesus Christ embodies the way that fits or is congruent with the truth. He is the one whom we may follow and, at the same time, become disciples of the way of God with the world. Therefore, knowledge of the one who embodies the way attests to the dynamic and multidimensional morphology of God focused in a human life. It indicates that divine reality comes to us as a dynamic power and presence in creative, sustaining, judging, and redeeming forms in and through our continuing experience of the one Christians call "the Son." Finally, Jesus Christ imparts the power of God that enables us to take up the life and walk in the way. He points to the divine power made perfect in weakness, and therefore knowledge of the one who imparts the power of God to change hearts attests to what Christians call "the Spirit." It indicates that divine reality is mediated as a dynamic, multidimensional power and presence in and through transforming experiences of reorientation and enlargement.

All three of these distinctive mediations are necessary for an adequate apprehension of divine reality, and they cannot be either separated or collapsed without damaging the integrity of the Christian community's vision of the divine dynamism in its bearing upon existence. Thus, the trinitarian symbolization of the distinctive mediations of divine presence contrasts with three unitarianisms. There is a unitarianism of the Father, which forgets the particularity of God's way in Jesus Christ and often fails to look for a change of heart. There is a unitarianism of the Son, which fails to attend to the dynamic power and presence of God in the world and often upholds a narrow and imitative legalism. There is a unitarianism of the Spirit, which dissolves into formlessness and often fails to engage the world. The doctrine of the Trinity stands against all three.

At the same time, the trinitarian doctrine upholds the dynamic unity of the Christian community's distinctive apprehension of God, because it insists upon the interrelation, interpenetration, and intersection of the dimensions of Father, Son, and Spirit in our experience. There is no experience of God as the dynamic power at work in the world that does not also point toward and overlap with apprehensions of human life in appropriately responsive relation to God as well as a heartfelt reorientation. For experience of God's order of grace indicates that the particular way of life characterized by love of God and neighbor is truly fitting, and it is clear that we can only be enabled to take up this life by a change of heart which lies beyond our own powers. There is no experience of the way of God focused in a personal human life that does not point toward and overlap with apprehensions of the power at work in all things as well as a change of heart. For the way of life characterized by love of God and neighbor is fitted to the contours of God's wider reign and empowered by the power to change hearts. There is no experience of the power of God that works inner reorientation and enlargement that does not also point toward and overlap with apprehensions of the dynamic power at work in the world and of personal life in appropriately responsive relation to that power. For this experience of reorientation and enlargement leads one to acknowledge God's dynamic order of grace and to walk in the way characterized by love of God and neighbor that comes to us in Jesus Christ.

In this manner, the trinitarian doctrine affirms that the three mediations of Father, Son, and Spirit are not accidental, and that the dynamic power disclosed to us in these distinctive mediations is indeed a unified, dynamic reality. The Trinity is a summary of the Christian community's distinctive discernment of God in which our interpenetrating and multidimensional experiences of God are affirmed as apprehensions of a single dynamic reality. It claims that, although God remains an unfathomable and even incomprehensible mystery, our apprehensions of God in space and time as a universal dynamic power and presence in three distinctive mediations of Father, Son, and Spirit furnish a true discernment of divine reality. In short, the Trinity insists that what is disclosed in our multidimensional experience is a single, unified, multidimensional, dynamic, and all-governing reality that always already stands in relation to all.[15]

One may affirm that, in all of these respects, the Trinity is crucial for the integrity of the Christian community's distinctive vision of God, and one may still believe that talk about eternal distinctions and relations among persons of the Trinity amounts to a speculative inference from our mediated experience. Indeed, I find it neither advisable nor particularly edifying to speak of God *in se* apart from our experience.[16] In this conviction I depart from certain strands of orthodoxy, although (I would argue) in a manner that retrieves the persistent discomfort with inordinate speculation of many of orthodoxy's chief representatives. Seeds of speculative reticence are present among the Cappadocians, who frequently stress "that the divine *ousia* is both inaccessible and unknowable."[17] Augustine admits that, when it comes to talk about three hypostases or persons, we are "speaking of things that cannot be uttered."[18] Although Calvin maintains that the three are "differentiated by a peculiar quality,"[19] he also pens the following admonition:

> Here, indeed, if anywhere in the secret mysteries of Scripture, we ought to play the philosopher soberly and with great moderation; let us use great caution that neither our thoughts nor our speech go beyond the limits to which the Word of God itself extends. For how can the human mind measure off the measureless essence of God according to its own little measure, a mind as yet unable to establish for certain the nature of the sun's body, though men's eyes daily gaze upon it? Indeed, how can the mind by its own leading come to search out God's essence when it cannot even get at its own? Let us then willingly leave to God the knowledge of himself.[20]

Both the multidimensionality and the unity of divine reality are indicated by our experience as it is informed by and refracted through the one who teaches the truth, embodies the way, and empowers the life. This, rather than the speculative reflections of metaphysicians, furnishes a true basis for trinitarian theology.

INCARNATION

Has one the right to use the word "incarnation" if one speaks of the mediated presence of God in Jesus Christ and refuses to speculate about eternal distinctions and relations in God? Certainly not in the sense of the two-natures doctrine understood as a substantive, meta-physical specification of how humanity and divinity co-inhere in Christ's person. Instead, the interpretation of the centrality of Jesus Christ offered here emphasizes the man Jesus as the brightest illus-tration of grace and, rather than rely on the notion of two natures, points to the emergence of a radical devotion to God in the man Jesus and the manner in which that devotion orients his life and ministry. Jesus Christ incarnates radical devotion to God.[21]

If, however, the basic issue here is more properly one of fun-damental aims than of language and conceptuality alone, then there are a number of respects in which this proposal stands in continuity with the classical tradition. As we have seen, Chalcedon may be re-garded as a kind of fractured dogma or symbolic statement which points toward the centrality of Jesus Christ rather than as a univocal statement about the physics of incarnation. My line of thinking about the presence of God in Jesus Christ, which is similar to Calvin's un-derstanding of the spiritual real presence of Christ in the Eucharist, requires that one relinquish the physicalist language and conceptuality of Chalcedon in favor of a more elusive vocabulary. By grace, the dynamic power and reality of God is truly present in the man Jesus as a constitutive and affecting principle of his personal identity. By grace, the man Jesus is a loving and efficacious symbol of God's reality, a symbol who, at one and the same time, participates in and is re-sponsive to the divine power that bears all things. For this reason, there is a disclosive relation between the symbolic form, orientation, or pattern of the one who teaches the truth, embodies the way, and empowers the life and the dynamic reality of the God who creates, sustains, judges, and redeems. Jesus Christ is the truly compelling disclosure of God as God always already stands in relation to all.[22]

Minimally speaking, Jesus Christ mirrors or reflects the reality of God. This underscores the idea that Jesus Christ, as a human being in authentic relation to God, is the one whose life is correspondent to God's reign of grace in the world in such a manner that the morphology of the way in him is fitted to the contours of the divine dynamism. Here, correspondence means something like the relationship between stamp and impress, only in this instance both stamp and impress are dynamic and living. Something like this is expressed by the Greek phrase *charakter tes hypostaseos autou* used with reference to Jesus Christ in Heb. 1:3. *Charakter* may be translated as impress, reproduction, or representation, so that the complete phrase might be rendered "an impression or representation of God's nature or reality."

In the phrase *hos estin eikon tou aoratou* (Col. 1:15), Jesus Christ is "the one who is the icon, image, or likeness of the invisible or unseen God." This metaphor is used in connection with the further affirmation that "in him all the fulness of God was pleased to dwell and through him to reconcile to himself all things" (Col. 1:19). Jesus Christ is the image or likeness of God in a sense that refers to the dependence on God of the whole creation, its order, continuing sustenance, reconciliation, and renewal. One might say that, because he is the *charakter* or *eikon* of God, knowledge of Jesus Christ is also knowledge of God in the fullness of God's dynamic relationality to all things.

This general line of thinking may be developed further by speaking of Jesus Christ as the wisdom, word, or Logos of God through whom all things were made and by whom all things are renewed (John 1:3). Among other things, this image points to the continuity between redemption in Jesus Christ and God's entire creation. Yet its force is not only to tell us that the covenant between God and humanity in Jesus Christ refers to a wider whole inclusive of all things; nor is it only to suggest that what is revealed in Jesus Christ about authentic human existence is of a piece with the proper tendency of all things under God. It is also to assert that the way of God with the world that comes to us in Jesus Christ is genuinely disclosive of the dynamic reality of God as God always already stands in relation to all things. In this sense, then, one who has seen this man has seen the Father.[23] The incarnational element or accent in my proposal is the affirmation that here the dynamic reality and power of God is manifest in a personal life.

Precisely as a real person whose life receives its dominant orientation from his heart's devotion to God, Jesus Christ is the one who participates in and discloses with compelling clarity the purposeful and dynamic reality of the God who always already stands in relation to all as Creator, Sustainer, Judge, and Redeemer. In Christ, people discern human life in appropriately responsive relation to God as well as the dynamic reality of God that always stands in relation to all. This resymbolization does not repeat Chalcedon. It does not require that one affirm the preexistence of Christ, and it does not entail speculative inferences about God *a se*. Neither can its more elusive and non-metaphysical vocabulary simply be read back into the field of past incarnational and adoptionist options. Nevertheless, I believe that it shares many of the fundamental aims of the classical tradition. For it too points toward the same mystery, namely, that Jesus Christ is the true light of the world, and that in him God was reconciling the world to God's self.

TRUE HUMANITY

Many traditional obstacles to Jesus' true humanity are removed when the concept of mediation is substituted for the doctrine of hypostatic union, since one need no longer contend with the dialectical difficulties of a relationship between two natures. Yet one difficulty remains concerning the suitability of Jesus for the work of redemption. Frequently, victory over sin has been thought to entail the further affirmation of Jesus' sinless perfection in a fashion that renders questionable his susceptibility to passionate conflict and growth.

Certainly this is a consequence of Anselm's classic theory of the atonement. Images drawn from Israel's sacrificial system are prominent in *Cur Deus Homo?* We read that humanity is "stained by the dirt of sin" and in need of washing or cleansing, and that Christ's death blots out the sins of others.[24] Nevertheless, the schoolman's central metaphors turn upon a more forthrightly Latin and legal image.

For Anselm, justice is to render someone that which he or she is due. To act unjustly is to injure another's honor, and restoration requires that the injured party's honor be satisfied. People owe God complete obedience in the sense that "every inclination of the rational creature ought to be subject to the will of God." But people are disobedient sinners, and have offended the infinite honor of God, which they can neither repay nor satisfy. Even if they now render complete obedience, they only render what they already owe in the first place and do not make reparation. What is needed to make satisfaction for sin is one whose complete obedience goes beyond what he owes. Such a one is the God-Man "giving himself up to death for the honor of God."[25]

When viewed as a whole, Anselm's theory is probably best understood as an eloquent testimony to redeeming grace. God alone removes the penalty for sin by God's free act of atonement in Jesus Christ. What I mean to underscore here, however, is the way that these legal metaphors encourage a focus on will and its immediate expressions in particular deeds. At critical points, Anselm actually collapses heart and will:

> This is the justice or rectitude of the will, which makes men just or upright in heart, that is, in will. This is the sole and entire honor which we owe God, and God requires from us. For only such a will does works pleasing to God, when it is able to act; and when it cannot act, it pleases by itself alone, since apart from it no work is pleasing.[26]

Therefore, for Anselm, the meaning of being without sin is clear. The suitability or fittingness of Christ for the task of redemption demands that the unambiguous obedience of his will be expressed directly and completely in all of his actions. Even the slightest movement in opposition to the will of God (e.g., "a single glance") demonstrates less than complete rectitude of will and sins gravely against God's honor.[27] Jesus Christ is the one whose will is entirely righteous in the sense that, when it can act, it always performs works that are unambiguously obedient and pleasing to God. While Christ had the power to commit a sinful act, for example, to tell a lie, "he could not lie against his will." Because he willed to honor God, he was not capable of willing to sin. So, in the sense of having the power to act, Jesus could sin, but in the sense of having the will, he could not.[28]

The problem, of course, is that Anselm's portrait of the man Jesus has a ring of unreality about it. How, on this theory, are we to account for the Gospel portraits of Jesus in the grip of passionate conflicts? How are we to envision the redeemer as a human figure who overcomes the destructive power of sin, if he cannot be portrayed as one who feels its force and "is tempted as we are" (Heb. 5:7)? Indeed, if Jesus is sinless in the sense of having no conflict in will or inclination, how can his example be at all relevant to creatures like ourselves?

As we have seen, a similar focus on will and obedient action seems present in Baillie's account of the incarnation. On the one hand, Jesus' choices and actions are genuinely contingent. On the other, these same choices and actions are also God's doing. Since, then, God's will determines all of Jesus' choices, all of Jesus' particular actions must be unambiguously obedient to God's will. This is not the place to enter a lengthy discussion of whether theories of the divine determination of particular human actions allow for a plausible account of human responsibility. But it is the place to observe that the undercurrent of determinism interjects into Baillie's portrait of Jesus a ring of unreality that is reminiscent of Anselm's doctrine. How, on Baillie's view, is it really possible to say that Jesus "learned obedience through what he suffered" (Heb. 5:7–9)?

Because my own view does not focus exclusively upon will and obedient actions, I believe it possible to offer an interpretation of Jesus' suitability or fittingness for the work of redemption that is more consistent with his genuine humanity. On my interpretation, Jesus remains unconquered in his devotion to God, and this is integral to his victory over sin. Yet it is also appropriate to surmise that his heart is something of a battleground on which devotion to God is challenged and comes into conflict with the inordinate pitch of other human affections. Like ourselves, Jesus harbors some instinct for self-preservation as well as desires for worldly success. He is loyal, not only to God but also to his historical community. In the Gospel narratives, these affectivities come into conflict with his dominant devotion to God. We need not and should not affirm Jesus' sinlessness in a sense that does away with all conflict.[29]

It is a feature of historical human life in the real world that conflicting loyalties cannot be adjudicated without passionate trade-offs, as when one's loyalty to one's family and its welfare comes into conflict with one's commitment to one's profession or with one's commitment to the welfare of the nation. Moreover, a given loyalty does not unambiguously dictate or determine every particular action or choice. Should an American patriot enlist in the army to fight in Vietnam? Should he or she take a desk job rather than a combat position? Should he or she work in the domestic political arena, perhaps even in an effort to resist the government's war effort? Similarly, even if we affirm that Jesus remains unconquered in his devotion to God, we need not and should not claim either that he experienced no conflict or that every one of his words and deeds was utterly determined by his devotion to God.

A number of occasions portrayed in the Gospels support this view. If Jesus is truly tempted in the wilderness, then we need to affirm that some interest in personal power and worldly success is doing battle in his heart with his dominant devotion to God. When he prays at Gethsemane, "Let this cup pass from me," we both can and should surmise that this is a scene of passionate conflict. Again, heart-rending conflict and doubt are depicted in some measure by his cry of forsakenness on the cross. Jesus' temptations, his prayers at Gethsemane, and his cry on the cross are episodes in a narrative that mean to express something other than the unambiguous determination of his every word and deed by his dominant devotion to God.

Indeed, the Gospels depict Jesus as one who shares with his social companions some measure of loyalty to the historical Jewish community, its traditions, insights, customs, and apparent prejudices. Most often, when these come into conflict with what is required by devotion to God, Jesus is portrayed as one who swiftly and appropriately orders his other loyalties in subordination to his dominant devotion, for instance, his willingness to associate with tax collectors and sinners, to heal on the Sabbath, or to heal the servant of a Roman soldier. But this is not unambiguously the case in every instance.

In the Gospel of Matthew, for example, Jesus is depicted as initially refusing to answer a Canaanite woman who seeks to have her daughter healed. As she continues to beg, he says, "I was sent only to the lost sheep of the house of Israel." When she kneels before him pleading, "Lord, please help me," Jesus replies, "It is not fair to take the children's bread and throw it to the dogs." Only after the woman says that even dogs eat crumbs that fall from their master's table does Jesus remark on her great faith and heal her daughter (Matt. 15:21–28).

Why does Jesus respond to the Canaanite woman like this? Why does he hesitate? Indeed, why does he demean the woman for being a Canaanite rather than an Israelite? The answer would appear to be that deep-seated loyalties to the Jewish community as well as prejudice toward its adversaries play an important role in the exchange. In the

Gospel of Matthew, this episode seems connected with the narrator's interest in the universality of the Great Commission and the subsequent mission of the church to all nations (Matt. 28:19–20). Certainly, we may conclude that the early church faced some ambiguity in the disposition of Jesus' ministry toward those outside of Israel, as a similar tension emerges between Peter, James, and Paul over the latter's mission to the Gentiles.

In any event, the writer of the Gospel of Matthew has narrated a story that is compatible with the suggestion that Jesus grows in his vision of what is required by his dominant devotion. It is compatible with the observation that, occasionally, conflicting loyalties may prevent him from envisioning every implication of his loyalty to God with utter clarity. Indeed, he may learn how to subordinate and order certain passions to his dominant devotion to the universal God only over time. But none of this means that Jesus' devotion to God is conquered; neither does it mean that the orientation of his life and ministry, even unto death on a cross, has been deflected. Quite the contrary, it means that, as Jesus walks in the way engendered by his dominant loyalty, both his devotion and his vision have been enriched by his encounters with others in God's world. For the narrator of Matthew's Gospel, all of this serves to instruct the church about its mission. Interestingly, however, the episode would not have been theologically possible had the narrator believed that the suitability of Jesus Christ for the work of redemption required the unambiguous determination of the redeemer's every word and deed.

It may be helpful to mention an analogy. The measure of a brother's devotion to his brother or sister is not that other loyalties to friends, wife, children, or profession never come into conflict with that devotion. Neither is it that these other passions and their conflicts with his devotion to sister and brother never lead him to see his responsibilities with something less than true clarity, or that they never lead him to perform an act or utter a word that expresses some confusion of heart or shortsightedness. The appropriate measure is rather in the more subtle and elusive orientation of his life as a whole, his dispositions, purposes, intentions, and characteristic actions. For every interaction with his sister or brother that does not clearly reflect his devotion to them, there may be many others that do. He may only learn how to negotiate his conflicting loyalties and responsibilities over time. But the uncharacteristic word or deed that reflects some momentary constriction of vision or of heart, some occasional fatigue or sorrow of soul, does not conquer the orientation of his life as one who loves his sister and his brother.

Jesus' temptations, his hard responses to the Canaanite woman, his prayers at Gethsemane, and his cry on the cross do not reverse or deflect the dominant orientation of his life, although they surely display his genuine humanity and show that he too grows in grace as well as in his understanding of his mission and its costs. It is a most telling feature of the Gospels that they do not shy away from episodes like these. For these episodes do not detract from the perception that here we have to do with a man whose heart and orientation overcome the forces of sin and evil. Indeed, they add to that perception. When we say that Jesus Christ is the true revelation of God and the true power of God to empower new life, we mean that he is these things precisely as a real man who experiences heartfelt conflicts that may sometimes come to expression in word and deed, but that conquer neither his heart nor the dominant orientation and direction of his life.

Thus, the suitability or fittingness of Jesus Christ for the work of redemption does not entail the belief that all of his particular actions are unambiguously determined. It means rather that radical devotion to God furnishes the dominant orientation and direction of his life and ministry, that he suffers crucifixion in the service of that radical devotion, and that still he comes today. Following Reinhold Niebuhr, one may judge that conflicting loyalties are a concomitant of finite and insecure existence, and that therefore "it is not possible . . . to assert the sinlessness of every individual act of any historical character."[30] Yet one may also affirm that in Jesus Christ there is a coherence of heart and life or of devotion and orientation, and that this coherence makes for another between the patterned dynamism of God and Jesus' affections and tendencies in action. Indeed, the Gospels invite us to discern just this subtle, almost aesthetic, quality or balance.

When we say that Jesus Christ is the true revelation or supreme mediation of God, we mean that real humanity, a person radically

devoted to God and whose life receives its orientation from that dominant devotion, is an appropriate way of manifesting God to people
within the conditions of space and time:

> Jesus is the Son of God not in spite of the historical form of his
> humanity, but exactly *in it*. The form which hides is at the same
> time the form of revelation. . . . Faith does not discern the divinity
> of Jesus Christ in some contra-human aspects of his career, which
> are hidden or interspersed with moments of his humanity, but it
> sees just this humility and weakness as the form of his true di-
> vinity.[31]

The *archegos* who is the brightest illustration of grace expresses in what
he does and endures, in the dominant orientation and disposition of
his life, the vector, direction, or morphology of God's grace at the
same time that he expresses the dominant devotion of his heart. Where
this ruling passion is most definitely displayed, so is the dynamic
reality of God, namely, in the whole of Jesus' life and ministry even
unto death on the cross.

6

The Christian Way

The Christian religion, if it has anything distinctive—and must not aspire to be the necessary outcome of *every* path of religious progress—is distinguished from other religions by its precept about the Way of Life.

—Charles Saunders Peirce

In this book, I have interpreted Jesus Christ as the one who teaches the truth, embodies the way, and empowers the life, as the mediator in whom the dynamic pattern of God's reality comes through with compelling clarity and in whom Christians discern the responsive pattern of human life conformed to God's purposes. Jesus Christ is the focal point for the guiding pattern of the historical Christian community. He is the center of meaning for a vision of God in relation to all things and for a manner of living that fits with that vision. He both engenders and interprets the identity and experience of the Christian community. This is what it means to say that Jesus Christ is central for the Christian community's experiences of God and of human life in appropriately responsive relation to God. Jesus Christ is the essential pattern or symbolic form that in-forms the Christian way of life.

THE CHRISTIAN WAY

This idea is not new. For ancient Israel, walking the way was closely connected with certain affections. "Blessed is every one who fears the Lord, who walks in his ways" (Ps. 128:1). It was also associated with guides to external behavior: "You shall teach them the statutes and the decisions, and make them know the way in which they must walk and what they must do" (Exod. 18:20). Christianity itself is called "the way" *(hodos)* in the Book of Acts. There, it is qualified in three instances: "the way of salvation" (16:17), "the way of the Lord" (18:25), "the way of God" (18:26).[1] For the Christian community, the way itself is come in Jesus Christ; to follow him is to walk in the way of God.

What sets off a way of life from just life or living is a kind of balance or quality that has to do with the bearing of things upon us. A way thematizes, orders, and shapes relations between self and others. It prioritizes varied values, wants, and desires. It aims at a kind of wholeness or coherence, an identity or vocation. It gathers life into a distinctive orientation.

The Christian way is multifaceted. It is responsive to God as Creator, Sustainer, Judge, and Redeemer. It is indissolubly connected with life together in Christ within a worshiping and ministering community. It is characterized by things such as repentance, humility, fairness, and justice, by special concern for the sick, the weak, the downtrodden, and the poor. Again and again, however, basic accounts of the Christian way return to a central theme: love of God and neighbor.

What this theme indicates is that the Christian way is one in which a distinctive apprehension of God qualifies and shapes human beings. In Christ, God is seen to be the dynamic power that always already stands in relation to all. Therefore, Christians believe that this power is faithful. No one separates us from God by threatening death or promising life. No principality or power, or thing present or to come, or height or depth cuts us off from this reality. In Christ, love for God is seen to be a passion that endures suffering and crucifixion. Therefore, Christians believe that this love is not easily shaken. God is the fountain of good in whom and for whom we hope, the cherished cause in whose service Christians stand willing to qualify and sometimes even to risk their own private interests. In Christ, both self and neighbor are seen to be creatures to whom God always already stands in faithful relation and who thus participate in a single, universal community. Therefore, Christians believe that love of God is indissolubly intertwined with love of neighbor. This comes through in Jesus' life and ministry, and it also is reflected in a signal obligation of the Christian life: "Let no one seek his own good, but the good of his neighbor" (1 Cor. 10:24); or, in less rigorous form, "Let each of you look not only to his own interests, but also to the interests of others" (Phil. 2:4). For the Christian community, these statements express a qualification of rational self-interest that is based in Jesus Christ and is integral to human life in appropriately responsive relation to God, a qualification that distinguishes the Christian way from many other ways of being human.[2]

Christianity is the specific way that is articulated in the story of God's dealings with Israel and focused in Jesus Christ. For those who walk in this way, "Jesus Christ is a symbolic form with the aid of which men tell each other what life and death, God and man are *like*." Jesus Christ furnishes a lens by which Christians understand the determiner of destiny, by which they interpret the self, and by which they apprehend the neighbor. In this way, he is for Christians an image "which gives form and meaning to their experience."[3]

Max Weber's understanding of religious ethics will help to enrich this. For Weber, a religious ethic clarifies ideas about humanity's place in the world, and these ideas imply more general conceptions of cosmic and moral order. By means of worship, preaching, teaching, and pastoral care, religious congregations then attempt to organize behavior in accordance with these conceptions. Or one might say that a religion furnishes a vision. Thus, Jesus Christ is the focal point for the Christian community's vision of the world as God's dominion and of ourselves as dependent creatures who dwell in that dominion. This vision may be regarded as a portrait of normative order, both cosmic and moral, with which the way embodied in Jesus Christ coheres. Acceptance of this vision entails belief, not only in the sense of affirming its cognitive validity, but also in the sense of a practical readiness to subordinate one's interests in its service. By means of worship, preaching, teaching, and pastoral care, Christian congregations equip people with this vision and encourage them to follow a certain path.[4]

On this interpretation, scripture may be regarded as a literary artifact in which the way comes to expression, and by means of which the community stabilizes its vision and practice.[5] The Bible is not so much a repository of timeless rules and beliefs as the timely, provoking expression of the way; its vision of God, world, and humanity; its object of loyalty in contest with other objects and loyalties; and its attitudes, dispositions, intentions, and characteristic actions. Like a classic novel that is drenched in the particularities of a place and time, the Bible articulates a vision and a manner of living for people in other times and places. It intensifies our sense of the bearing of things upon us and brings that bearing into focus under the rubric of God's dominion. It chronicles, symbolizes, and suggests a way of relatedness that is responsive to that dominion. Particularly in and through its portrayals of and statements about Jesus Christ, the Bible points to the common third or accompaniment in all of our relations with others, or what Richard R. Niebuhr calls "God-Ruling." In order to apprehend "this wider field and our commerce with it," says Niebuhr, "we must first awaken to it" both intellectually and affectively. Then we begin to understand how the Bible exercises authority "augmenting and directing men's lives," because it interprets, represents, and focuses this wider field.[6]

A "chicken-and-egg" question arises at this juncture. Is the Bible primarily a document that expresses preexisting experiences, or is it primarily a document that creates a world and thus constitutes the experiences of the community?[7] Questions such as this one have provoked illuminating discussions. Those who argue that scripture is primarily expressive of experiences have explored vital senses in which biblical symbols refer to experienced realities, and have suggested how these symbols may be tested for their adequacy to our experiences. Those who have argued that scripture is primarily productive of experiences have explored important senses in which tradition shapes perception, character, and identity, and also have suggested that, among those formed by Christian tradition, there is a predisposition toward the confirmation of biblical meanings in their experiences. Yet there is little reason to regard a stark choice between these alternatives as either inescapable or final. To say that the Bible is only an expression of preexisting experiences fails to take sufficient account of how people are shaped or conditioned by the historical communities and traditions in which they participate. To say that the Bible is only a linguistic framework that constitutes the community's experiences is to forget other factors, both biological and social, that condition the ways in which Christians envision the world, as well as the power of certain experiences and alternative visions to call occasionally into question inherited interpretative frameworks. The interplay between text and experience is richer, more complex, and more dialectical than either alternative allows. The Bible expresses and points toward the experiences of the religious community in the world. The Bible also functions as an inherited framework that helps to interpret and engender the community and its experiences. Authority lies *both* in scripture's ability to shape the lives and experiences of Christians *and* in the confirmation of its meanings in the experiences of Christians.

The classic literatures of other traditions function similarly. They furnish historical communities with foci of stability for vision and practice because they too articulate particular ways of life together with appropriate qualifications of human affect and action. They too grapple with the question of our response to the bearing of things upon us and the question of our relations with others. A scriptural tradition offers people resources for construing the powers bearing down upon them and for responding in fitting ways.[8] It therefore becomes a basis, by means of the community's interpretation and reappropriation, for an identity, a generalized orientation or pattern of behavior.[9]

Therefore, two marks of a way or manner of living are distinctiveness and historical particularity. Ways of life are distinctive; many of their salient features may be compared with and distinguished from those of other ways and orientations. So one may compare the Christian way, its vision, dominant devotion, characteristic attitudes, dispositions, intentions, and actions with those of other life patterns, with, for example, the ways of Stoicism or of Islam. Ways of life are historically particular; they emerge in specific social and historical contexts. So the Christian way is indissolubly connected with the stories of Israel and of Jesus Christ that are remembered, portrayed, preserved, and interpreted by a particular historical community. The Islamic way is borne similarly, as are other ways.

THE CHRISTIAN WAY
AND OTHER WAYS OF BEING HUMAN

Recognition that ways of life are both distinctive and historically particular points to the unavoidable role of a tradition. People do not become who they are; they are not formed in their sensibilities, identities, vocations, or orientations apart from specific communities and communal histories. Therefore, who people are and the specific paths that they follow cannot be known apart from the particularities of a historic tradition.

Yet this recognition should not be confused with the assertion that there are no commonalities among different ways. In fact, there appear to be general patterns that are fit for humans.[10] This judgment, which furnishes a basis for understanding commonalities among people and their distinctive ways, will come as no surprise to a Christian theologian who believes that God as Creator, Governor, and Redeemer is a present, active, and universal power. For this affirmation implies a common and responsive third that accompanies all of our particular relations and interactions, and therefore that all ways of being human will share certain characteristics to the extent that they are shaped by the bearing of this common reality upon them.

So, for example, Augustine regards the virtues as common elements of human affection, and believes that they receive their particular stamp or direction from the subject's love or devotion to some object or objects. Patience, then, is that virtue by which people suffer evils for the sake of the good that they love. In the Christian way, it becomes the disposition to endure hardships for the sake of God and God's purposes. Yet one may be patient also in the service of some other devotion that anchors another way of living.[11] Again, in his treatise on *The Catholic and Manichean Ways of Life,* after having argued that the Christian way is based in devotion to God in Christ as the true good, the bishop of Hippo claims that the four cardinal virtues may be understood as various dispositions of love of God. In general terms they may be defined as follows:

> Temperance is love giving itself wholeheartedly to that which is loved, fortitude is love enduring all things willingly for the sake of that which is loved, justice is love serving alone that which is loved and thus ruling rightly, and prudence is love choosing wisely between that which helps it and that which hinders it.

The Christian, the Roman patriot, and the Manichee are all alike in this respect. Each participates in these general patterns of disposition to the extent that they are well-formed in their respective orientations.

The differences come with *what* they love, with their different objects of devotion that are distinctively portrayed by their various traditions, and with the distinctive ways in which these objects qualify their dispositions. Thus, in the Christian way the four virtues are defined with reference to God:

> Temperance is love preserving itself whole and unblemished for God, fortitude is love enduring all things willingly for the sake of God, justice is love serving God alone and, therefore, ruling well those things subject to man, and prudence is love discriminating rightly between those things which aid it in reaching God and those things which might hinder it.[12]

For Augustine, different ways of being human are defined by their different objects of devotion. Indeed, in *The City of God,* he points to something like that temperance which preserves itself for God in the citizen who truly loves Rome, something like that fortitude or courage which endures all things for God, that justice which serves God alone, and that prudence which discriminates between those things that are helpful and unhelpful.[13] Yet it is important to understand that no actual individual is formed by the virtues *in general.* Strictly speaking, the general description of the virtues amounts to an abstraction. People are oriented in history only by particular determinations of the virtues in devotion to a specific, historically envisioned object.

Another illustration of general patterns of commonality among different ways is the "second table" of the decalogue (Exod. 20:12–17; Deut. 5:16–21). Thomas Aquinas identifies these statutes with the law of nature that is known to all people.[14] John Calvin notes general agreements between the second table and the laws of the nations.[15] Indeed, observations such as these are not confined to Christian theologians. In a recent philosophical introduction to ethics, Arthur Dyck includes a discussion of "the ancient code of the Mosaic covenant, for which there are counterparts in other religions and cultures." He justifies this inclusion on the grounds that it introduces the reader to constraints that safeguard human associations that "are requisite to there being any form of community or cooperative action among people."[16]

One may regard these moral requisites as "generalizations about the moral values and principles which provide the conditions *sine qua non* for human personal and social life."[17] Obviously, any life that is appropriate for our highly social species needs to involve some form of community or cooperative social life. Human beings need to participate in communities, and general patterns that make social cooperation possible will be common to ways that are fit for humans. In terms of the Christian vision, these patterns may be regarded as general characteristics of human society that are shaped by the bearing of divine power upon all people.

Once again, however, it is important to see that these patterns do not constitute a "natural" way of being human alongside other, "non-natural" ways. People are not formed by these patterns precisely because these patterns are so very general. Real life and actual identity involve specifics. Just because the more determinate possibilities that cohere with the general patterns fit for humans are so varied and so rich, there must be some selection. That is why actual ways of life that are fit for humans are always bound up with particular historical communities, their literatures, their ethos, and their polities. Thus people are formed not by marriage or the family *in general* but by particular forms of these institutions in specific societies whose roles are filled by individuals with their own peculiar histories, habits, and characteristics. The general and common patterns that are fit for humans come to expression in and through the highly varied historical particulars of specific communities, their present circumstances, and their traditions.

This brings us to a second, related point of no small importance. Some ways appear to be less fit for humans than others. It is true that human beings may be formed in a variety of ways and that the plurality of historical traditions and cultures is evidence of this. There is no single way of being human. Nevertheless, human beings are not infinitely plastic. If they were, then any conceivable way would do just as well as any other. But such plainly is not the case. While there is a significant range of appropriate ways of being human, this range is not unlimited.

This, again, should come as no surprise to Christian theologians. Certain forms of gnostic dualism, for example, were judged deficient by the Christian community in earlier centuries. The main theological issues surrounding this judgment are well known. Some Gnostics distinguished God the Redeemer from the Creator, believed that Jesus Christ was sent by the Redeemer to release us from the material realm, and that the way of salvation amounts to the soul's escape from created nature. By contrast, the church came to insist that the Redeemer and the Creator are one, that Jesus Christ is the Son of the all-governing Father, and that the way of God in Christ does not entail the denegration of created nature. The fundamental disagreement, then, concerned both vision and life, or different judgments concerning what is truly valuable and appropriate for human beings. What the church gained from this controversy was not only a strengthened ability to envision God's rule over nature and history, but also (and correspondingly) a strengthened appreciation for the goodness of created human nature engaged in the sensible world. The church's negative judgment was that the dualistic vision of certain Gnostics, with its portrait of the human being as an essentially spiritual being, supported a way of living that, in its contempt for the sensible life of the body, was less fit for humans than the catholic way.[18] Similarly, when Augustine takes the Manichees to task because their belief that the soul becomes entangled in evil flesh at birth leads them to abhor the procreation of children, the issue is more than speculative. The Manichees envision two gods, an evil creator and a good redeemer. For them, the true good that one loves is limited to the realm of spirit and in conflict with the material world. What the bishop of Hippo is suggesting is that the way of life engendered by this devotion and its dualistic vision runs counter to the grain of our natures and is therefore less than fit for humans.[19]

Another manner of living that is less than fit for humans, and one with reference to which the historical record of the Christian community is considerably less satisfying, is slavery. Patterns of kinship and family exist in all known human societies precisely because, in virtue of certain species-specific characteristics, people are emotionally predisposed toward long-term partnerships and toward caring for their children. Moreover, just because the given constitution of human beings presents so many varied faculties and potentialities, it is critical that acceptable social orders afford individuals a significant range of options for social expression, achievement, and participation. But in this country until the middle of the nineteenth century, blacks suffered an order in which their families were forcibly separated and their options for social expression and achievement severely limited. Where so many powerful and basic predispositions are systematically thwarted, the fabric of human life is badly torn. A theology that takes the given biological constitutions of people in God's world with the same seriousness with which Augustine and others once took the sensible life of the body, will have little difficulty arriving at the judgment that slavery amounts to a manner of life that is less than fit for humans. Because the institution of slavery plainly is so unresponsive to basic dimensions of created human nature, it conflicts with the affirmation of God's lordship over nature and history. Indeed, this is true of all grossly oppressive social policies and orders to the extent that they too systematically and inordinately limit possibilities for the social expression and development of many common and basic human faculties and predispositions.

To summarize, a way of life may be regarded as a historically particular pattern of attitudes, dispositions, intentions, and actions that is anchored by a dominant devotion to some object or objects, coheres with a vision of the world and humanity's place in it, and forms or orients human beings in a distinctive manner. Jesus Christ is the central symbolic form that in-forms the particular vision and pattern of the historical Christian community. Furthermore, some ways are more fit for humans than others, and there are points of commonality among them. Indeed, in virtue of its discernment in Jesus Christ of God's universal dominion over nature and history, the Christian community has reason to be actively concerned about the human integrity of the Christian way, and also about the relative fitness for humans of diverse social orders and practices.

CONVERSION, CONSCIENCE, AND IMAGINATION

None of this should be surprising to a Christian theologian. Classical Christianity has long maintained that God's redeeming grace and creative, providential works are integrally related, that created human nature is good, and that sin is not our nature but its derangement. Redeeming grace regenerates, restores, and redirects fallen humanity; it does not destroy or replace created human nature. Indeed, created human nature, its faculties and predispositions, constitutes a gift from God that may be taken as an indication of God's purposes. Only those who wish to reconsider the extreme dualisms that have long been decisively rejected by the Christian community will be uncomfortable with these beliefs, and part of the force of these beliefs is to insist that ways of life that are fit for humans are more responsive to the dynamic reality of God than are ways that are unfit for humans.

This does not mean that the Christian way is merely the republication of the general patterns that are fit for humans.[20] Indeed, no historical way is. As the one who teaches the truth, embodies the way, and empowers the life, Jesus Christ both moves and guides people along a specific path—one characterized by devotion to God and love of neighbor, dispositions such as humility, intentions such as caring for the weak, and actions such as healing the sick. To accomplish this, he does battle with tendencies toward egoism, pride, and violence. "That is *metanoia:* not in the first place thinking about one's own needs, problems, sins, and fears, but allowing oneself to be caught up into the way of Jesus Christ, into the messianic event, thus fulfilling Isaiah 53."[21] The way that comes to us in Jesus Christ is a particular pattern that qualifies and redirects human affect and action. It does not spontaneously grow or develop from the affective inventory of the human species. So far as we know, there is no evolutionary inevitability about it. Instead, it is both articulated and called forth by the particularities of a specific history and preeminently by a particular figure in that history. Moreover, in the experience of the Christian community, there is little reason to expect either smooth or untroubled transitions among people from the skewed devotions and misdirected ways that historically entrap them to the way, the truth, and the life in Christ. To walk in the Christian way requires a change in ourselves.

We might talk about this change somewhat differently by exploring the manner in which the Christian way qualifies or redirects human consciences. Conscience is a name for the practical reflection of human subjects. This reflection yields complex judgments concerning the appropriateness or inappropriateness of attitudes and actions to one's dispositional make-up and to one's vision of the environment. Moreover, the importance of this sort of reflection is difficult to overestimate. Our dispositional make-ups present us with manifold and sometimes conflicting tastes, wants, and needs. Similarly, our

environments furnish a variety of stimuli as well as varied and sometimes mutually exclusive avenues for expression and action. Conscience operates at the multifaceted intersection of our selves and our
environments. It is the reflective, affective, and imaginative personal
center that lends a certain balance or structure to our lives in the world.

Interestingly, this is not just an optional extra. Human beings
have need of lasting character, personal style, or at least of some measure of continuity, if they are to lead lives that cohere at all and are not
constantly at crossed purposes. Conscience is reflection in the service
of our interest in making sense out of life, an interest that correlates
with our human need for coherence. Because conscientious judgments
are responsive to this need, they carry with them a certain force,
weight, or authority. Because they are near and dear to our hearts,
they are not easily manipulated by others or even by ourselves.

Clearly, when they are understood in this way, our consciences
and their judgments are socially conditioned. This is because the bases
for our conscientious determinations, our dispositional make-ups, and
our imaginative visions of the environment are themselves shaped by
interactions with significant others (e.g., parents and siblings), given
patterns of association (e.g., divisions of labor, schools, and profes-
sions), and by the mental assets of our cultures (e.g., arts, sciences,
histories, religious ideas, causes, and values). Also, it is difficult to
ignore psychological evidence for a relationship between various (often
childhood) experiences and the affective capacities of people to be
loving, trusting, hopeful, purposive, dependable, caring, and so forth.
The multiplicity and variety of the specific personal and social relationships in which people stand is a significant factor making for diversity in, and sometimes also the malformation of, their consciences
and their moral judgments.

Still, we need not conclude that our dispositional make-ups and
imaginative visions are the exclusive products of our social relations
and personal decisions. There are biological bases for many human
affections—for tendencies to attend to the responses of others, toward
social cooperation, and toward aggression, and for impulses of sexual
attraction, maternal affection, social acceptance, friendship, and
achievement.[23] Many of these predispositions are relatively open, and
need to be ordered or drawn out in specific ways by our cultures if

we are to have any opportunity at all to lead coherent lives. Here, indeed, the forces of "nature" and "nurture" go hand in hand. Yet our deep-seated predispositions are not infinitely plastic; neither are they easily circumvented or eliminated by any social order. The vast majority of known societies appear responsive to many of the requirements and strictures that our predispositions place upon efforts at social cooperation, for example, tendencies toward aggression checked by prescriptions against violence and murder, impulses of sexual attraction ordered by forms of marriage, needs for parental guidance, care, and affection supported by forms of the family. Similarly, many of our personal decisions about basic values also appear responsive to our biologically funded predispositions. So, for example, in most human societies, parents generally feel especially bound to care for their young children, and what is perceived as the maltreatment of young children is almost universally disapproved. Our deep-seated human predispositions, then, are factors that make for certain broad commonalities in conscientious human judgments.

We also should note an important imaginative capacity in human beings, that is, the ability of persons to project themselves into another's place or circumstances. No doubt, this capacity has its limits. It is enhanced by friendship as well as by knowledge of the other's situation. It is hampered by lack of information or common experiences. It is socially shaped, and is critically dependent upon our culturally conditioned visions of what another's circumstances are. The imaginative capacity also may be psychologically skewed, for example, by paranoia or by disproportionate feelings of self-aggrandizement. But *that* it is a quite general human capacity seems apparent from the virtually universal appeal of certain forms of art and literature. (Remember the first time you "identified with" a character in a novel by, for instance, Charles Dickens or Joseph Conrad?) Indeed, even in cultures where one group's members are systematically discouraged from projecting themselves into another's circumstances, some do anyway. (Remember the first time you read *The Adventures of Huckleberry Finn?*) This imaginative capacity contributes to the almost universal approbation among human beings of certain standards of equity or fairness. (How would you feel if you were treated like Huck's friend Jim?)

Now, if an interpretation such as this one holds up, then while we cannot maintain that there is a "natural" conscience that operates exactly the same way in all people, we can affirm that there are bases for certain limited agreements in the conscientious judgments of historically conditioned human subjects. No real person's conscience reduces merely to broad commonalities, and yet commonalities necessarily come to expression in the particular ways in which our biologically given predispositions and capacities are drawn out by our historical communities.

Moreover, the complexities of nature and nurture also shed light on the relationship between conscience and the Christian way. The Christian way pronounces neither an unqualified "yes" nor an unqualified "no" over human consciences, nor does it unilaterally create a Christian conscience that is wholly incommensurate with the consciences of others. Instead, it affects our dispositional make-ups and imaginative visions by enlarging these dimensions of our persons toward love of God and neighbor, and thereby it reorients the resources for our lines of practical reasoning. The Christian way reorients the heartfelt and visionary foundations for our consciences and our characters. It has a visceral effect upon personal identity because it alters our wants and desires as well as our visions of ourselves and our companions.[24]

How is this so? A key point is that the way that comes to us in the historical Christian community is differentiated and characterized by the particular pattern or symbolic form of Jesus Christ. Without rehearsing all that has been said on this score in previous chapters, here we should review a few relevant items. Jesus Christ articulates a vision of God and God's creation. Therefore, we envision ourselves and our companions as creatures who share a common dependence upon a single Creator, Sustainer, Judge, and Redeemer. He articulates a rule of fairness that occupies a significant place among the mental assets of the Christian community. "So whatever you wish that men would do to you, do so to them; for this is the law and the prophets" (Matt. 7:12). The Christian way therefore functions positively to support and extend our imaginative tendencies to put ourselves in another's place. Jesus Christ comes to us in the form of a servant, which occupies a foundational place among the mental assets and polities (or patterns of association and interaction) of the historical Christian community.

> You know that those who are supposed to rule over the Gentiles lord it over them, and their great men exercise authority over them. But it shall not be so among you; but whoever would be great among you must be your servant, and whoever would be first among you must be slave of all. For the Son of man also came not to be served but to serve, and to give his life as a ransom for many (Mark 10:42–45).

The Christian way therefore functions positively to support and enlarge our affective tendencies to attend to others, their goods and interests.

Other dispositional qualities should be mentioned here as well. The way that comes to us in Jesus Christ commends humility, patience, and kindness. It also commends certain directions in action concerning the use of force; the honoring of promises; treatment of the poor, the weak, and the outcast; healing the sick; faithfulness in marriage; and so on.

By contrast, then, the way that comes to us in Jesus Christ also calls into question many of our impulses toward selfishness, rivalry, and aggression. It challenges lapses of constricted vision when, in our practical reasonings, we fail to take into account the wider society of God and neighbor. Yet this does not mean that Jesus Christ performs radical surgery upon our natures. Impulses toward selfishness, rivalry, and aggression, as well as tendencies toward jealousy, envy, impatience, revenge, and so on, remain as aspects or dimensions of our tempers. Only now, our task of practical reasoning becomes how to criticize, restrain, or redirect these impulses and their socially formed expressions in a fashion that accords priority to love of God and neighbor.

The main point is that the way that comes to us in Jesus Christ enlarges our hearts and our visions toward love of God and neighbor. Indeed, love of God and neighbor go together, since hearts and minds oriented toward God are no longer curved in upon self and self's private interests alone. One corollary of this view is that to walk in the Christian way requires a change in ourselves; Jesus Christ teaches, embodies, and empowers a way of life anchored in devotion to God.

This qualifies or rebalances our dispositional make-ups and our characters. Another corollary is that one of the main factors making for the unreliability of human consciences is the chronic tendency of human hearts and minds toward misorientation or constriction. People in every culture and psychological state tend to be inordinately curved in upon themselves. This, indeed, is the radical and pervasive power of sin, and although Jesus Christ breaks sin's death-dealing dominion, sin does not for that reason cease to dwell within us. It too remains a potent, negative force infecting the tempers of Christian hearts and minds.

CENTRALITY VERSUS ISOLATION

This brings us to a final question, namely, the relationship between the centrality of Jesus Christ and exclusivity, an issue that arises whenever one considers Christian discipleship and that takes on increasing importance wherever Christians encounter diverse cultures, varied artistic, literary, and philosophical works, scientific knowledge, and other religions. With respect to discipleship, there are good reasons to understand Jesus Christ more subtly than is allowed by portraits of him as the exclusive norm for a life of appropriate responsiveness to God. For one thing, Jesus himself points to a multidimensional divine reality that comes to us in and through a variety of media and not only in and through him. In this sense, he is not a closed norm, but one that points to the reality of God in a wide range of human experiences. This is part of the meaning of references in his teaching to the historical experiences and the law of Israel, to the moral excellence of some who stand outside of the official religious community (e.g., the Good Samaritan), and to natural phenomena. Moreover, the Christian community persistently has applied at least some images to interpret the significance of Jesus Christ that connect him with a similarly wide range of experiences, such as prophet, king, and high priest, perfect sacrifice, wisdom of God, Logos. Finally, contemporary knowledge of the variety of factors that influence the sorts of persons we become and so shape the lives and experiences of Christians indicates that knowledge of and loyalty to Jesus Christ cannot function as the exclusive architect of their moral identities. Experience in Jesus Christ of God and of human life in appropriately responsive relation to God "is refracted through the prism of what a person is becoming as the result of other" influences and experiences as well.[25] To be a disciple of the way of God in Jesus Christ is not strictly to imitate Jesus, but rather as a biologically constituted and socially shaped individual at one's particular place and time to be in-formed in one's responsiveness to God and to others by the symbolic pattern of Jesus Christ as articulated in the New Testament.

The centrality of Jesus Christ does not mean that we should insulate Christian theology from conversations with cultural expressions in the arts, literature, or philosophy, or with scientific studies and other religions. Nevertheless, a number of contemporary theologians find it tempting to embrace a kind of sectarian confessionalism that isolates Christianity, its way, and its vision.[26] Isolation can be supported in a variety of ways. One may adopt a distrustful attitude toward the theological and moral relevance of all cultural expressions on the grounds that all cultural insights are "fallen." Then all sources of knowledge and values are radically subordinate to the Christian community's (unfallen?) reading of the historic Christian tradition and its portrait of Jesus, which now becomes the exclusive norm for all interpretations of the Christian way. Or one may endorse a theory of religion that understands historically particular traditions and their literatures to be productive of unique and incommensurate experiences of the world. Christian theology then sets for itself the task of absorbing the universe into its (unique) biblical world, and does not ask whether its interpretation of the Christian vision is adequate to other interpretations of human experiences. Or one may adopt an epistemological theory that holds that rationality is pluralistic. This may support the view that Christian theology is interpretation in a constricted sense that refers only to a discrete, radically inward, and personal context of life and logic that bears no relation to scientific interpretations of human life and the world.[27]

The attractions of isolation are clear, and perhaps one should expect them to become especially tempting whenever the basic meanings and values of a tradition are called into question. From the university to the seminary and from the pulpit to the pew, isolation ensures a strong sense of distinctiveness and identity that remains untroubled by many of the intellectual challenges of the modern world. Indeed, it may very well be that a heightened longing for unassailable and radically distinct identity is symptomatic of contemporary life in mobile, pluralistic, postindustrial cultures, and that the current popularity of isolationist stances in Christian theology reflects this situation. But such untroubled identity can be purchased only at great price. Not only does isolation jeopardize the intelligibility of Christianity in the modern world and render the question of Christianity's claims to truth deeply problematic, but it often leads to interpretations of the Christian vision that are less than faithful to many of the distinctive features of historical Christian tradition.[28]

Particularly when it occurs among those who mean to represent trinitarian movements within historic Christianity, the new isolationism appears to be a defensive attempt to protect one's tradition that can only end by losing it. For isolationism forgets to look for mediations of the dynamic power and presence of God in and through experiences of nature, history, and society as God's dominion. It therefore mutes the affirmation of God's dynamic power and presence in the world. Indeed, the assertion of a meaningfully positive relationship between creation and redemption depends upon a robust affirmation of the universal lordship over nature and history of the God disclosed in Jesus Christ. Yet this affirmation is more fragile than at first it may appear. When (whether in virtue of a theory of religion, an epistemological theory, or because sin is too simply identified with culture) one asserts that sources of insight other than the historical Christian community and its tradition are entirely unreflective of God's purposes, what is qualified is the sense that all things stand within the universal community of divine responsiveness. The insulation of the Christian way from science and culture therefore threatens the very basic apprehension of Christian piety that what comes to us in Jesus Christ is the reality of the all-governing God who always already stands in relation to all. It forgets that Jesus himself points to a multidimensional divine reality which comes to us in a wide range of human experiences through a variety of media.

So to say that Jesus Christ is central for the Christian way does not mean that he is the only relevant source for our vision of God, humanity, and world. That should be apparent from the classic affirmation (authorized by the Gospel portraits of Jesus' ministry) that

God in Christ is not a reality who meets us in Christ alone, but rather one who always already stands in responsive relation to all. That Jesus is not the only relevant source for our vision of God should be apparent from the continued reliance of both the New Testament communities and subsequent Christian tradition on the witness of the Hebrew scriptures (also authorized by the Gospel portraits of Jesus). From the perspective of the Christian community, the truth that Jesus teaches, the way that he embodies, and the life that he empowers fulfill and complete the apprehension of God in relation to all things that is articulated in Israel's vision. Moreover, the authors of Israel's wisdom as well as classical Christian theologians such as Augustine, Aquinas, Calvin, and Jonathan Edwards, do not hesitate to consult the wider compass of nature and history in their efforts to understand God and humanity's place in God's world. To say that Jesus Christ is central for our vision of God and of human life in appropriate relation to God is neither to deny nor disparage the relevance or the importance of other apprehensions and sources of knowledge in piety's quest to understand God and the place of human beings in God's creation. Rather, other apprehensions and the knowledge we gain from them are to be ordered and construed in light of the sovereign reality disclosed to us in and through the way, the truth, and the life. That is the continuing and also relatively subtle intellectual challenge of Christian piety. Jesus Christ is the focal point for the guiding pattern of the historical Christian community. In faithful reasoning about the power that governs all things and our appropriate responses to that power, our perception of Jesus becomes a key image or symbolic form for our vision of the whole.[29]

What does this mean for conversations and dialogue with scientific inquirers, artists, philosophers, and representatives of other religious traditions? Christians have theological grounds for participating in such conversations and for considering them to be truly important. The Christian community's apprehension of God in Christ as the sovereign ruler of all things directs our attention to a wide range of human experiences to determine whether and how the presence and purposes of this sovereign power may be discerned and made intelligible.[30] Such apprehension therefore encourages engagement with the world. To amend a statement made by Dietrich Bonhoeffer in the midst of his struggle against Nazism, "The reality of God discloses itself only by setting me entirely in the reality of the world; but there I find the reality of the world always already created, sustained, judged, and reconciled in the reality of God."[31]

On this score, the older study of divinity that once dominated theological education in America was more profound than many recent seminary curricula. Pious learning was connected with studies in languages, rhetoric, grammar, and natural philosophy, that is, mathematics, physics, biology, astronomy.[32] The indispensability of the historical Christian tradition was clearly recognized, even as theological education refused to be seduced into believing that this tradition is the exclusive source of insight. Thus, for Edwards, the lively sense of God's sovereignty meant that God clearly is more than a textual reality and led to a changed perspective on nature. Edwards believed that scripture sanctioned revelation through nature and that both scripture and nature were languages of God.[33] When he wrote his outline for "A Rational Account of the Main Doctrines of the Christian Religion," he noted that the preface to that work should "shew how all arts and sciences, the more they are perfected, the more they issue in divinity, and coincide with it, and appear to be as parts of it."[34]

Nevertheless, if, from the perspective of the Christian community, conversations with philosophy, the arts, sciences, and other religions are truly important, their purpose is not to move toward a common faith or world theology.[35] The point is rather more modest, namely, to foster understanding, so that Christians may better comprehend God in relation to all things and so that they may better know where they share more or less common insights with others and where they differ. Christians both can and should enter interdisciplinary and interreligious discussions because they have both distinctively confessional and more generally public reasons for wanting to construe all things in their appropriate relations to the God disclosed to them in Jesus Christ, and for wanting to foster community among all people. They enter these discussions as people who acknowledge the universal Lord of all, the one who always already stands in responsive relation to all. And they participate in these discussions as people who envision that reality by the particular light that has come to them in their history.

There is nothing to prevent Christians who participate in such conversations from pursuing commonalities, or even asking whether there is not also among others something like the way, the truth, and the life that has come to them in Jesus Christ. Likewise, they may ask whether there are not analogues among other visions to the distinctively Christian apprehension of divine reality.[36] It may happen that through interdisciplinary and interreligious discussions Christians will find possibilities disclosed to them for better understanding the historical apprehension of God that has come to them as well as for better understanding their own lives in Christ. Certainly, this has long been recognized to have been the case with Augustine's appreciation of Roman history and Aquinas's reading of Aristotle. It also has been true of many conversations with Marxist philosophy among contemporary theologians in Latin America.[37]

It must also be admitted, however, that one may meet in another religion, another person, or among the philosophers, the arts, and the sciences possibilities for viewing the world and God in relation to it that cannot be used to enrich one's vision in Jesus Christ, but instead call that vision into question. It is possible that one may encounter a disclosure of God and/or vision of the world that is, in one's judgment, both antithetical and superior to what one discerns and knows in Jesus Christ. This, of course, is the possibility of conversion away from the way, the truth, and the life to some other skein of vision and devotion. To admit this possibility is, in fact, to comprehend what the centrality of Jesus Christ finally means. It is also to understand what one means when one calls the man Jesus the supreme mediation of God's reality and the supreme example of human life in appropriately responsive relation to God. For if it happens that Jesus Christ no longer furnishes the focal point or lens through which one's other experiences of God, self, and world are construed; if it happens that one can no longer be oriented in life by devotion to the Creator, Governor, and Redeemer of all things apprehended in and through Jesus Christ; if it happens that the symbolic form of Jesus Christ no longer in-forms one's identity and vocation, then one is no longer a Christian.

Jesus Christ is the way into God's kingdom that has come to us with compelling clarity in the history of the Christian community. There may be other ways, but this is the one we know. He is the one in our experience who teaches the truth about God in relation to all things. He is the one in our experience who guides and empowers a way of life that coheres with the truth. It is perhaps not for finite, historically conditioned, and wayward creatures like ourselves to make absolute pronouncements upon the ultimate value of the ways that have apparently come to others in their histories. In any event, as those whose hearts have been altered in Christ, we haven't the hearts to follow other ways, and only an unforeseen change of heart could move us in some other direction.

> Whatever other men may say we can only confess . . . that through our history a compulsion has been placed upon us, and a new beginning offered us which we cannot evade. We must say with St. Augustine: "Walk by him the Man, and thou comest to God. By him thou goest, to him thou goest. Look not for any way except himself by which to come to him. For if he had not vouchsafed to be the way we should all have gone astray. Therefore he became the way by which thou shouldest come. *I do not say to thee, seek the way. The way itself is come to thee: arise and walk.*"[38]

Appendix

The Historical Development
of Trinitarian Doctrine

I interpret the Trinity in Chapter Five as a symbolization of both plurality and unity in the Christian community's discernment of God. My purpose here is to suggest how aspects of the historical development of trinitarian doctrine may be understood in these terms.

Speaking very generally, there were two basic approaches to the Trinity during the patristic period. The west started from the premise of divine unity and moved toward a recognition of the plurality of Father, Son, and Spirit in the economy of redemption. The east began with the plurality of Father, Son, and Spirit and moved toward an increased appreciation for divine unity rooted in an identity of divine operations in the contingent realm.

Tertullian, who spoke of one substance *(substantia)* distributed into three persons *(personae)* in the economy of revelation, took an important step toward the recognition of divine triplicity in the west. The term "person," however, did not carry the now familiar meaning of an independent, self–conscious personality, but signified a role, mask, or presentation of an individual. Tertullian therefore envisioned one divine power that comes to us in three forms or expressions. In the east, Origen of Alexandria, who forged an impressive synthesis of neo-Platonic philosophy and Christianity, took a different approach. Origen maintained that the Father is alone God in the strict sense. The Father is the absolute unity or monad from which the multiplicity of beings proceeds. The eternally begotten Logos or Son, who is the express image of the Father, mediates between the monad and the multiplicity of the temporal realm; the Spirit is the highest being brought into existence by the Word. Father, Son, and Spirit are therefore three distinct hypostases, and there is, for Origen, plurality in our experience of the divine in space and time. Nevertheless, there is also a kind of unity, since the wills of the Father and the Son are virtually identical, and the Son shares the Father's divinity derivatively, by participation.[1]

Tertullian came into conflict with representatives of older western approaches who feared the pluralist implications of his teaching. "Modalistic Monarchians" maintained that the Son is distinct in name only, being a projection or extension of the Father.[2] Sabellius, who apparently became modalism's most sophisticated architect, claimed that God is a monad (called "Son-Father") who, by a process of enlargement or "dilation," projects himself into modes of self-expression like rays from the sun, first as Son and then as Spirit. Tertullian objected that this approach entails the blasphemous teaching of patripassianism; in his projection as Son, the Father suffers. As is often pointed out, Tertullian's objection condemns modalism's failure to protect the impassibility of the Father. Interestingly, it also indicates modalism's inability to articulate sufficient plurality in our apprehension of God in Jesus Christ under the conditions of space and time. For the Gospel portraits of Jesus' references to the Father as a reality distinct from himself (including the Lord's Prayer), his struggle with the Father's will for him at Gethsemane, and his words on the cross indicate a more radical multidimensionality in the Christian community's experience of God than is indicated by the dilations of a monad.

The continuing vitality of Arianism in the east threatened the unity of the Christian community's apprehension of God. Somewhat like Origen, the Arians portrayed God the Father as the monad or strict essential unity. They were then compelled to depict the Son as a separate subordinate being who mediates between the utterly transcendent, impassible Father and the temporal, multiplicitous creation. Since the impassible Father is alone God in the strict sense, this meant that experience of Jesus Christ is experience not of God but of an intermediate reality.

The debate moved in somewhat different directions after Nicea, whose revolutionary *homoousios* clause aligned orthodoxy against Arian portraits of the Son as a separate being subordinate to the Father. Indeed, decisive subsequent expressions of orthodox trinitarianism no longer employed the monad or paradigm of strictly simple unity as a fundamental concept.

The Cappadocians—Basil of Caesarea, Gregory of Nyssa, and Gregory of Nazianzus—pushed eastern thinking toward a recognition of greater unity. Father, Son, and Spirit were conceived as hypostases in which the one God distributes or presents itself. Yet because there is identity in their several operations in our experience, we infer the unity of the divine nature. Thus, the unity of the divine *ousia* follows from the unity of divine action rather than from an insistence on the paradigm of simple oneness. Emphasis falls not on mere numerical unity but on a unity of nature signaled by the unity of divine operations.[3]

In the west, Augustine fashioned a vocabulary that makes it possible to affirm both the unity and plurality of the deity. He is uneasy with terms such as *persona* and "hypostasis," and he suggests that the unity of God will be more clearly expressed if we speak of three real or subsistent relations in God that act "as one principle" in relation to the contingent world. However, since each has the divine nature in a particular manner, the multidimensionality of our experience is preserved by attributing to each an appropriate role in the temporal realm.[4] It is this apprehension—that in our experience Father, Son, and Spirit act as a single principle and also that each has an appropriate and distinctive role—which I have tried to depict in my own terms in Chapter Five.

Notes

1. WHAT IT MEANS TO STAND IN A LIVING TRADITION

1. Maurice Wiles, "Christianity without Incarnation?" in *The Myth of God Incarnate*, ed. John Hick (Philadelphia: Westminster Press, 1977), 1–10; and John B. Cobb, Jr., *Christ in a Pluralistic Age* (Philadelphia: Westminster Press, 1975), 17.

2. José Míguez Bonino, *Doing Theology in a Revolutionary Situation* (Philadelphia: Fortress Press, 1975), 2.

3. Hans Küng, *On Being a Christian*, trans. Edward Quinn (New York: Doubleday & Co., 1976), 129.

4. Edward Schillebeeckx, *Jesus: An Experiment in Christology*, trans. Hubert Hoskins (New York: Seabury Press, 1979), 29.

5. Richard R. Niebuhr, *Experiential Religion* (New York: Harper & Row, 1972), xii–xiii, 1–14.

6. James M. Gustafson, "The Vocation of the Theological Educator," *Austin Seminary Bulletin* 101, no. 7 (1986): 13–26.

7. Many of the basic concepts and contentions of this chapter are drawn from Ernst Troeltsch's "What Does 'Essence of Christianity' Mean?" in *Ernst Troeltsch: Writings on Philosophy and Religion*, ed. and trans. Robert Morgan and Michael Pye (London: Gerald Duckworth & Co., 1977), 124–79. I also have learned more than I can adequately acknowledge here from David Tracy's discussions of "the religious classic" in *The Analogical Imagination: Christian Theology and the Culture of Pluralism* (New York: Crossroad, 1981), 99–229.

8. These polarities might be stated in a variety of ways and probably are not exhaustive. They appear as elements of H. Richard Niebuhr's analysis of basic stances in Christian ethics in *Christ and Culture* (New York: Harper & Row, 1975). I have discussed them in *Meaning and Method in H. Richard Niebuhr's Theology* (Washington, D.C.: University Press of America, 1982), 98–125.

9. B. A. Gerrish, *Tradition and the Modern World: Reformed Theology in the Nineteenth Century* (Chicago: University of Chicago Press, 1978), 181.

10. The primary aim of Christian theology is to serve God and neighbor. Where this is attempted in full recognition of our creaturely limits and sinful tendencies, it will be apparent that theology does not secure an

absolute certainty that we are correct and others are wrong. One submits one's theological work for the critical scrutiny of the wider Christian community, a community whose life continues to be informed by the originating and subsequent classics of scripture and church history. This community may determine the range of positions that it finds legitimate, although those charged with this responsibility by one or another institution do well to remember that their task is to establish a *range* of legitimate positions rather than a single, self-consistent, and detailed theology. Within this community, one has the right to expect that measure of tolerance and humility that appropriately follows the recognition that no one occupies a place of such authority as to control the meaning of the scriptures.

11. Edward Shils, *Tradition* (Chicago: University of Chicago Press, 1981), 1–33.

12. I use the terms "occasionalism," "individualism," and "utopianism" here, as also the term "traditionalism" later on, merely to signify general and illustrative types.

13. The relationship between Christian theology and other disciplines is complex. I have outlined my understanding of this relationship in "Christian Theology and Other Disciplines," *Journal of Religion* 64, no. 2 (1984): 173–87.

14. Lisa Sowle Cahill makes a similar proposal in *Between the Sexes: Foundations for a Christian Ethics of Sexuality* (Philadelphia: Fortress Press; Paramus, N.J.: Paulist Press, 1985), 4–7.

15. See H. Richard Niebuhr, *The Meaning of Revelation* (New York: Macmillan Co., 1960), 44–45; and idem, "Introduction to Biblical Ethics" in *Christian Ethics: Sources of the Living Tradition,* ed. Waldo Beach and H. Richard Niebuhr (New York: Ronald Press Co., 1955), 4–5, 10–11. Niebuhr here compares the Bible as the "book of Christian beginnings" with the foundational documents of other communities.

16. Gerrish (*Tradition and the Modern World,* 7, 183) says that it is typical of liberal Protestantism that scripture no longer serves as the exclusive critical norm. Theology takes on a "mediating" character because it opens the door to other points of reference besides scripture and attempts to mediate among them. The appropriating and transforming of the past or the *development* of doctrine is what theology is all about. Its statements are to be constantly retested by the dual norm of fidelity to the tradition and intelligibility in the modern world. My own approach, in some sense, is a mediating one.

2. INTERPRETING THE CLASSICAL TRADITION

1. See Joseph Sittler's *The Anguish of Preaching* (Philadelphia: Fortress Press, 1966), 30–31. Hans W. Frei argues a similar point in *The Identity of Jesus*

Christ: The Hermeneutic Bases of Dogmatic Theology (Philadelphia: Fortress Press, 1975), 35–52.

2. James D. G. Dunn, *Christology in the Making: A New Testament Inquiry into the Origins of the Doctrine of the Incarnation* (Philadelphia: Westminster Press, 1980), 266–67. Dunn quotes from Schillebeeckx's *Jesus: An Experiment in Christology,* trans. Hubert Hoskins (New York: Seabury Press, 1979), 53.

3. For reconstructions of the Apostles' Creed, I have relied upon J. N. D. Kelly, *Early Christian Creeds,* 3d ed. (New York: McKay, 1972), 131–66. For a different reconstruction, see A. C. McGiffert, *The Apostles' Creed* (New York: Charles Scribner's Sons, 1902), 84–100.

4. Kelly, *Creeds,* 131–66; McGiffert, *The Apostles' Creed,* 13–14.

5. Kelly, *Creeds,* 182.

6. Ibid., 181–83, 194–96.

7. Charles Joseph Hefele, *A History of the Christian Councils from the Original Documents,* ed. and trans. William R. Clark, 2d ed. (Edinburgh: T. & T. Clark, 1894), 1:260. Hefele draws his remarks from descriptions of the emperor's letter offered by Eusebius in his *Life of Constantine* and Socrates' *Ecclesiastical History.* Evidently, Constantine's own theology was not particularly sophisticated, and his grasp of the doctrinal issue at Alexandria was rather limited. See Aloys Grillmeier, S.J., *Christ in the Christian Tradition,* trans. John Bowden, 2d ed. (Atlanta: John Knox Press, 1975), 1:261–64.

8. Robert M. Grant, *Augustus to Constantine: The Thrust of the Christian Movement into the Roman World* (New York: Harper & Row, 1970), 236–40.

9. Hefele, *Christian Councils* 1:279–81.

10. Kelly, *Creeds,* 205.

11. However, Grant (*Augustus to Constantine,* 241) notes that a year later the two dates were still different.

12. Hefele, *Christian Councils* 1:375–435. See also Grant's *Augustus to Constantine,* 241–42. The practice of celibacy among the clergy was by no means uniform in the church at this time, and the west tended to be more stringent than the east. There was also disagreement over whether the third canon of Nicea required those who were already married to suspend conjugal relations with their wives upon ordination.

13. John H. Leith, ed., *Creeds of the Churches: A Reader in Christian Doctrine from the Bible to the Present,* rev. ed. (Richmond: John Knox Press, 1973), 31.

14. Grillmeier, *Christ in the Christian Tradition,* 266; Kelly, *Creeds,* 227–28.

15. Kelly, *Creeds,* 213, 235–36, 243.

16. Ibid., 285–87.

17. Grillmeier's *Christ in the Christian Tradition,* 272, 274–554, gives an exhaustive account of these developments.

18. *The Bazaar of Heraclides,* trans. G. R. Driver and L. Hodgson (London: Oxford University Press, 1925), 207; cited by Grillmeier in *Christ in the Christian Tradition,* 516. It should be noted, however, that Nestorius himself gives some evidence of concern for a substantial or ontological unity of Christ's person "after the same manner as the manner of the Trinity."

19. Grillmeier, *Christ in the Christian Tradition,* 326–27.

20. "Second Letter of Cyril of Alexandria to Succensus," *Documents in Early Christian Thought,* ed. Maurice Wiles and Mark Santer (Cambridge: Cambridge University Press, 1975), 67.

21. "First Letter of Cyril of Alexandria to Succensus," cited by John Meyendorff in *Christ in Eastern Christian Thought* (Tuckahoe, N.Y.: St. Vladimir's Seminary Press, 1975), 20.

22. Grillmeier, *Christ in the Christian Tradition,* 544; Kelly, *Early Christian Doctrines,* 2d ed. (New York: Harper & Brothers, 1960), 342.

23. R. V. Sellers, *The Council of Chalcedon: A Historical and Doctrinal Survey* (London: SPCK, 1961), 201–11.

24. Meyendorff, *Christ in Eastern Christian Thought,* 29.

25. Grillmeier, *Christ in the Christian Tradition,* 545.

26. Hefele, *Christian Councils* 3:198; Sellers, *Council of Chalcedon,* 57–58; Kelly, *Doctrines,* 331.

27. Hefele, *Christian Councils* 3:188.

28. Grillmeier, *Christ in the Christian Tradition,* 524.

29. Sellers, *Council of Chalcedon,* 61–62.

30. Hefele, *Christian Councils* 3:203–4.

31. S. G. F. Berry, ed., *The Second Synod of Ephesus, together with Extracts Relating to It* (Dartford, Eng.: Orient Press, 1881), 3–10.

32. J. A. Dorner, *History of the Development of the Doctrine of the Person of Christ,* vol. 1, 2d div., trans. D. W. Simon, vol. 10 of *Clark's Foreign Theological Library,* 3d ser. (Edinburgh: T. & T. Clark, 1865), 85.

33. Hefele, *Christian Councils* 3:265–67; Dorner, *Person of Christ,* 90.

34. Hefele, *Christian Councils* 3:268–73; Sellers, *Council of Chalcedon,* 97–98.

35. Hefele, *Christian Councils* 3:277–78.

36. Ibid., 284.

37. Sellers, *Council of Chalcedon,* 103.

38. Ibid., 108–10; Hefele, *Christian Councils* 3:295–319.

39. Hefele, *Christian Councils* 3:328–29.

40. Ibid., 342–53; Sellers, *Council of Chalcedon,* 116–23.

41. Hefele, *Christian Councils* 3:353–55, 410–20.

42. Sellers, *Council of Chalcedon,* 114.

43. Understandably, the letters of Cyril and Leo, which the council accepted as orthodox at its second session, are considerably more detailed with respect to the question of how Christ's humanity and divinity operated in the incarnation.

44. Grillmeier, *Christ in the Christian Tradition*, 552–53; Bernhard Lohse, *A Short History of Christian Doctrine: From the First Century to the Present*, trans. F. Ernest Stoeffler (Philadelphia: Fortress Press, 1966), 94.
45. Reinhold Seeberg, *Text-Book of the History of Doctrines*, trans. Charles E. Hay, 2 vols. (Grand Rapids: Baker Book House, 1958), 1:279–82.
46. Jaroslav Pelikan, *The Growth of Medieval Theology (600–1300)*, vol. 3 of *The Christian Tradition: A History of the Development of Doctrine* (Chicago: University of Chicago Press, 1978), 53–58.
47. Ibid., 142.
48. Thomas à Kempis, *The Imitation of Christ*, ed. Harold C. Gardner, S.J. (Garden City, N.Y.: Doubleday & Co., 1955), 69–72. See also Francis De Sales, *Introduction to the Devout Life*, trans. John K. Ryan (New York: Harper & Brothers, 1950), 32, 133, 170, 183–85.
49. Kirchenpostille, *D. Martin Luthers Werke*. Kritische Gesamtausgabe (Weimar, 1883), 10.I.1:47, trans. and quoted by Jaroslav Pelikan, *The Reformation of Church and Dogma (1300–1700)*, vol. 4 of *The Christian Tradition: A History of the Development of Doctrine* (Chicago: University of Chicago Press, 1984), 156. In the first edition of his *Loci*, 63, as quoted by Robert S. Franks, *The Work of Christ: A Study of Christian Doctrine* (London: Thomas Nelson & Sons, 1962), 318, Philipp Melanchthon echoes a similar sentiment: "This it is to know Christ, to know His benefits, not, as they (the schoolmen) teach, His natures, and the modes of the incarnation."
50. John Calvin, *The Institutes of the Christian Religion*, ed. John T. McNeill, trans. Ford Lewis Battles, vols. 20 and 21 of *The Library of Christian Classics* (Philadelphia: Westminster Press, 1960), 1.13.3–5.
51. Ibid. 2.13.2; 2.15.1.
52. B. A. Gerrish, *The Old Protestantism and the New: Essays on the Reformation Heritage* (Chicago: University of Chicago Press, 1982), 206–7.
53. See Karl Holl's remarks about Luther's *Anfechtungen* in *What Did Luther Understand by Religion?*, ed. James Luther Adams and Walter F. Bense, trans. Fred W. Meuser and Walter R. Wietzke (Philadelphia: Fortress Press, 1977), 74ff.
54. John H. Leith, "Introduction," *John Calvin: The Christian Life* (New York: Harper & Row, 1985), vii.
55. Calvin, *Institutes* 2.12.1–3; 2.14.
56. Donald G. Bloesch, *Essentials of Evangelical Theology* (New York: Harper & Row, 1982), 1:133. See also H. R. Mackintosh, *The Doctrine of the Person of Jesus Christ*, International Theological Library, series ed. Charles A. Briggs (New York: Charles Scribner's Sons, 1924), 230–46.
57. Kelly, *Doctrines*, 375, 390–92. Augustine tends to identify the mediating function with Christ's humanity, though he also says that "we could not be redeemed, even through the one mediator . . . if he were not also God." See Augustine, *The Enchiridion on Faith, Hope and Love*, ed. Henry Paolucci (Chicago: Henry Regnery, 1961), 126.

58. Eugene R. Fairweather, ed., *A Scholastic Miscellany: Anselm to Ockham* (New York: Macmillan Co., 1970), 150–51.

59. John Frederick Jansen, *Calvin's Doctrine of the Work of Christ* (London: James Clarke & Co., 1956), 26–29, 33–34. This last reference cited in Jansen is to Augustine, *Ennaratio in Psalm 26,* 2 MSL, 199.

60. Jansen, *Calvin's Doctrine of the Work of Christ,* 16–17, 20, 26, 30; Edward D. Morris, *Theology of the Westminster Symbols* (Columbus, Ohio: Champlin Press, 1900), 325–44.

61. Thomas Aquinas, *Summa Theologiae,* trans. Fathers of the English Dominican Province, 2 vols. (New York: Benziger Brothers, n.d.), 3.22.1; 3.26.1.

62. Calvin, *Institutes* 2.15.2, 4, 6.

63. Morris, *Theology of the Westminster Symbols,* 325.

64. Jansen, *Calvin's Doctrine of the Work of Christ,* 39–59; *Calvin's New Testament Commentaries,* ed. David W. Torrance and Thomas F. Torrance (Grand Rapids: Wm. B. Eerdmans, 1963), 12:34–35, 54–57, 86–87.

65. Augustine, *The Enchiridion on Faith, Hope and Love* 49.58–60; 108.126; Kelly, *Doctrines,* 393–94; *St. Augustine: Commentary on the Sermon on the Mount,* trans. Denis J. Kavanagh, vol. 11 of *The Fathers of the Church* (Washington, D.C.: Catholic University of America Press, 1951), 19–22.

66. Cited from Luther's *Commentary on Galatians* (1535), 5:8, by Jaroslav Pelikan in *Reformation of Church and Dogma,* 164.

67. Gerrish, *The Old Protestantism and the New,* 197; David W. Lotz, *Ritschl and Luther: A Fresh Perspective on Albrecht Ritschl's Theology in the Light of His Luther Study* (Nashville: Abingdon Press, 1974), 35; Walter Rauschenbusch, *A Theology for the Social Gospel* (Nashville: Abingdon Press, 1945), 27–28.

68. E.g., Shirley Jackson Case's claim in *The Historicity of Jesus* (Chicago: University of Chicago Press, 1912), 310, that traditional christology is not supported by critical inquiry into the historical life and teaching of Jesus and that "a modern worldview cannot adopt this type of metaphysical speculation."

69. Rauschenbusch, *A Theology for the Social Gospel,* 150–51.

70. Friedrich Schleiermacher, *The Christian Faith,* ed. H. R. Mackintosh and J. S. Stewart (Philadelphia: Fortress Press, 1976), §95; Friedrich Schleiermacher, *The Life of Jesus,* ed. Jack C. Verheyden (Philadelphia: Fortress Press, 1975), 81–87.

71. Adolf Harnack, *History of Dogma,* trans. Neil Buchanan (New York: Dover Publications, 1961), 4:106.

72. Paul Tillich, *Systematic Theology* (Chicago: University of Chicago Press, 1951), 2:142; John B. Cobb, Jr., *Christ in a Pluralistic Age* (Philadelphia: Westminster Press, 1977), 168; Schubert M. Ogden, *The Point of Christology* (New York: Harper & Row, 1982), 8.

73. Karl Barth, *Church Dogmatics,* ed. G. W. Bromiley and T. F. Torrance, trans. G. W. Bromiley et al. (Edinburgh: T. & T. Clark, 1957), 4/1:7; Emil Brunner, *The Christian Doctrine of God,* vol. 1 of *Dogmatics,* trans. Olive Wyon (Philadelphia: Westminster Press, 1950), 14, 23, 122, 139.

74. Reinhold Niebuhr, *The Nature and Destiny of Man: A Christian Interpretation* (New York: Charles Scribner's Sons, 1941), 2:70.

75. Adolf Harnack, *What Is Christianity?* trans. Thomas Bailey Saunders (New York: Harper Torchbooks, 1957), 235.

76. Schleiermacher, *The Christian Faith,* §98.

77. Barth, *Church Dogmatics* 1/2:151ff., 164ff.

78. Reinhold Niebuhr, *The Nature and Destiny of Man* 2:70–76.

79. Maurice Wiles, "Christianity without Incarnation?" in *The Myth of God Incarnate,* ed. John Hick (Philadelphia, Westminster Press, 1975), 4.

80. John Hick, "Jesus and the World Religions," in *The Myth of God Incarnate,* 178.

81. Schubert M. Ogden, *The Point of Christology,* 8–9.

82. G. W. H. Lampe, "Christian Theology in the Patristic Period," in *A History of Christian Doctrine,* ed. Hubert Cunliffe–Jones with Benjamin Drewery (Edinburgh: T. & T. Clark, 1978), 136. See also Walter Lowe, "Christ and Salvation," in *Christian Theology: An Introduction to Its Traditions and Tasks,* ed. Peter Hodgson and Robert H. King (Philadelphia: Fortress Press, 1982), 202. Jürgen Moltmann interprets Cyril to mean that the second person of the Trinity assumes the flesh as impersonal human nature: "But if the centre in Christ which forms his person has a divine nature, how can it be said of the whole divine and human person of Christ that he suffered and died forsaken by God?" Moltmann says that it is precisely the question of whether the predicates of the divine nature can be ascribed to the human nature and vice versa that was addressed with increasing subtlety by medieval theologians through the doctrine of *communicatio idiomatum.* He argues that Martin Luther was able to use this doctrine "to overcome the intellectual barrier that arose out of the doctrine of the two natures," although Luther's resolution requires a less technical and precise use of the term "God" (Jürgen Moltmann, *The Crucified God: The Cross of Christ as the Foundation and Criticism of Christian Theology,* trans. R. A. Wilson and John Bowden [New York: Harper & Row, 1974], 231, 234–35). Regardless of whether one judges Luther to have succeeded in this effort, it is important to note that intellectual barriers indeed have arisen out of the two-natures doctrine. See D. M. Baillie, *God Was in Christ: An Essay on Incarnation and Atonement* (New York: Charles Scribner's Sons, 1948), 85–94.

83. Anthony T. Hanson and Richard P. C. Hanson, *Reasonable Belief: A Survey of the Christian Faith* (Oxford: Oxford University Press, 1980), 92–106; Alan Richardson, *Creeds in the Making: A Short Introduction to the History*

of *Christian Doctrine* (Philadelphia: Fortress Press, 1981), 90. Richardson favors a more personalistic understanding of the incarnation and notes that "the ancient theologians were sorely handicapped by the limitations of the language in which they wrote."

84. Baillie, *God Was in Christ,* 83.
85. H. Richard Niebuhr, *The Responsible Self: An Essay in Christian Moral Philosophy* (New York: Harper & Row, 1963), 163.

3. JESUS CHRIST AND THE NEW TESTAMENT

1. Albert Schweitzer, *The Quest of the Historical Jesus: A Critical Study of Its Progress from Reimarus to Wrede,* trans. W. Montgomery (New York: Macmillan Co., 1968), 401.
2. Rudolf Bultmann, *Theology of the New Testament,* trans. Kendrick Grobel (New York: Charles Scribner's Sons, 1951), 1, 6.
3. Ibid., 3.
4. Ibid., 33.
5. Rudolf Bultmann, *History and Eschatology: The Presence of Eternity* (New York: Harper Torchbooks, 1957), 151–52.
6. Karl Barth, *The Christian Life: Church Dogmatics IV, 4: Lecture Fragments,* trans. Geoffrey W. Bromiley (Grand Rapids: Wm. B. Eerdmans, 1981), 35.
7. Karl Barth, *Church Dogmatics,* trans. G. W. Bromiley et al., ed. G. W. Bromiley and T. F. Torrance (Edinburgh: T. & T. Clark, 1961), 3/4:24–25, 30.
8. Barth, *The Christian Life,* 42–44.
9. Barth, *Church Dogmatics* 4/2:535, 533.
10. Ibid., 547.
11. Ibid., 546–53.
12. Ibid., 1/1:6, 10, 72.
13. Schubert Ogden, *The Point of Christology* (New York: Harper & Row, 1982), 71–72.
14. Mary Midgley, *Heart and Mind: The Varieties of Moral Experience* (New York: St. Martin's Press, 1981), 3.
15. Thus we speak of "behavioral predispositions," meaning that persistent, genetically based affectivities come to expression in patterns of behavior. See Joseph Lopreato, *Human Nature and Biocultural Evolution* (Boston: George Allen & Unwin, 1984), 335.
16. The word "generally" is important. It is no argument against the connection between genetically funded emotional constitutions and certain patterns of behavior that an occasional buffalo remains stationary or that an occasional human is wholly noncommunicative. These are aberrant patterns of behavior precisely because they differ so sharply from the general patterns that characterize their respective species and are likely to

severely hamper individuals in adapting to their environment. Such behavior may often have deep roots, some of which are genetic.

17. A social environment is made up of both society and culture. These cannot
be separated, though they may be distinguished for the purposes of discussion. By "culture" I mean, in the words of Clifford Geertz, "an historically transmitted pattern of meanings embodied in symbolic forms, a
system of inherited conceptions expressed in symbolic forms by means
of which men communicate, perpetuate, and develop their knowledge
about and attitudes toward life" (Geertz, *The Interpretation of Cultures* [New
York: Harper & Row, 1963], 78). By "society" I mean institutions or
persistent patterns of interaction. Examples might be the representative
form of government in the United States, or specific forms of the family
in different societies.

18. Lopreato, *Human Nature and Biocultural Evolution,* 78.

19. Mary Midgley, *Beast and Man: The Roots of Human Nature* (Ithaca, N.Y.:
Cornell University Press, 1978), 297.

20. Lopreato, *Human Nature and Biocultural Evolution,* 147–48.

21. Midgley, *Beast and Man,* 260–62.

22. Friedrich Schleiermacher, *The Life of Jesus,* trans. S. M. Gilmour, ed. Jack
C. Verheyden (Philadelphia: Fortress Press, 1975), 6.

23. William McFeeley, *Grant* (New York: W. W. Norton, 1981), 244.

24. Robert Alter, *The Art of Biblical Narrative* (New York: Basic Books, 1981),
116–17. I have made use of ideas and insights from Alter's book throughout
this section.

25. Ibid., 116–30.

26. Ogden, *The Point of Christology,* 53.

27. See Rudolf Bultmann, "Primitive Christian Kerygma and the Historical
Jesus," in *The Historical Jesus and the Kerygmatic Christ: Essays on the New
Quest for the Historical Jesus,* trans. Louise Pettibone Smith and Erminie
Huntress Lantro (New York: Charles Scribner's Sons, 1958), 27ff.

28. See Marjorie B. Chambers, "Was Jesus Really Obedient unto Death?" in
Journal of Religion 50, no. 2 (April 1970): 135.

29. Ernst Käsemann, *New Testament Questions of Today,* trans. W. J. Montague
and Wilfred F. Bunge (Philadelphia: Fortress Press, 1969), 64. I have added
the words in brackets.

30. Jonathan Edwards, *Charity and Its Fruits: Christian Love as Manifested in the
Heart and Life,* ed. Tryon Edwards (Carlisle, Pa.: Banner of Truth Trust,
1969), 83–84, 152; idem, "The Excellency of Christ," in *The Works of
Jonathan Edwards,* memoir by Sereno E. Dwight, rev. Edward Hickman
(Edinburgh: Banner of Truth Trust, 1974), 1:680–82. See also Augustine,
"The Christian Life" and "Patience" in *The Fathers of the Church,* trans.
Mary S. Muldowney, S.S.J. et al., ed. Roy J. Deferrati (New York: Fathers
of the Church Inc., 1952), 14:19–20, 39–40, 243.

31. H. Richard Niebuhr, *Christ and Culture* (New York: Harper & Row, 1975), 19. For Schleiermacher, Jesus' God-consciousness gives impulse to all of his life experiences. See Schleiermacher, *The Christian Faith*, ed. H. R. Mackintosh and J. S. Stewart (Philadelphia: Fortress Press, 1976), §93.

32. Stanley Hauerwas, *A Community of Character: Toward a Constructive Christian Social Ethic* (Notre Dame, Ind.: Notre Dame University Press, 1981), 44. See also Hans Frei, *The Identity of Jesus Christ: The Hermeneutical Bases of Dogmatic Theology* (Philadelphia: Fortress Press, 1975), 141–42.

33. H. Richard Niebuhr, *The Responsible Self: An Essay in Christian Moral Philosophy* (New York: Harper & Row, 1963), 157.

4. THE TRUTH, THE WAY, AND THE LIFE

1. C. H. Dodd, "Jesus as Teacher and Prophet," in *Mysterium Christi: Christological Studies by British and German Theologians*, ed. C. K. A. Bell and Adolf Deissmann (New York and London: Longmans, Green & Co., 1930), 53–55; idem, *The Founder of Christianity* (London: Collier–Macmillan, 1970), 53–79; Joseph A. Fitzmyer, S.J., *The Gospel according to Luke I–IX*, vol. 28 of *The Anchor Bible*, ed. William Foxwell Albright and David Noel Freedman (Garden City, N.Y.: Doubleday & Co., 1981), 149, 213–15, 218.

2. Maurice Wiles makes a similar point with reference to "the essence" of the Christian form of life when he observes that "both that we are and what we have it in us to become are not of our own contriving." *Faith and the Mystery of God* (Philadelphia: Fortress Press, 1982), 63–64.

3. This is probably a good place for me to say something about my understanding of theological language. My preference is for images such as God's realm and God's dominion. Expressions such as these signal my indebtedness to Reformed Calvinism. They also accord with the judgment that God is best indicated as the affecting power mediated to us in and through the multiplicitous totality of our environment. In this, I agree with Richard R. Niebuhr, "Religion, Faith, and Power," in *Frontline Theology*, ed. D. Peerman (Richmond: John Knox Press, 1967), 147. "If I must choose one word now to indicate the meaning of the word 'God,' it is power. (Of the several alternatives available today, such as being, act, love, this one seems to me to be the most universally significant.)" Niebuhr also shows that this choice reflects a good deal of New Testament language, especially in the Gospel of Mark. See idem, *Experiential Religion* (New York: Harper & Row, 1972), 118–24.

   I take God-talk to point toward affecting dimensions of divine power in our experience. So, for example, I think that Jesus' use of the word "Father" points toward the steadfast faithfulness of God, toward God's forceful authority, and also toward what some older prayers called God's "fatherly discipline" or "corrective judgment." Many of these meanings might be suggested in contemporary English by the words "father," "mother," or even "parent," although we should not assume an exact equivalence between the faithfulness, authority, and judgment of God in our experience and the behavior of either fathers or mothers.

4. See, for example, Jonathan Edwards's *Charity and Its Fruits: Christian Love as Manifested in the Heart and Life,* ed. Tryon Edwards (Carlisle, Pa.: Banner of Truth Trust, 1969), 5.

5. Karl Barth, *Church Dogmatics,* trans. G. W. Bromiley et al., ed. G. W. Bromiley and T. F. Torrance (Edinburgh: T. & T. Clark, 1961), 3/2:217.

6. Thomas Aquinas, *Summa Theologiae,* trans. Fathers of the Dominican Province (New York: Benziger Brothers, n.d.), 1–2, 100.10.

7. David W. Torrance and Thomas F. Torrance, eds., *Calvin's New Testament Commentaries* (Grand Rapids: Wm. B. Eerdmans, 1963), 3:36–39.

8. Edwards, *Charity and Its Fruits,* 5, 176–77.

9. Augustine, "Homilies on 1 John" in *Augustine: Later Writings,* ed. and trans. John Burnaby (Philadelphia: Westminster Press, 1955), 264.

10. Barth, *Church Dogmatics* 4/2:522–52; James M. Gustafson, *Christ and the Moral Life* (Chicago: University of Chicago Press, 1976), 205–11. On the matter of possessions, see also Martin Hengel, *Property and Riches in the Early Church* (Philadelphia: Fortress Press, 1974), 23–30.

11. Stanley Hauerwas, *Vision and Virtue: Essays in Christian Ethical Reflection* (Notre Dame, Ind.: Fides/Claretian, 1974), 187ff.

12. *Babylonian Talmud,* Shabbat, 31ac.

13. *St. Augustine: Commentary on the Sermon on the Mount,* trans. Denis J. Kavenaugh, vol. 11 of *The Fathers of the Church* (Washington, D.C.: Catholic University of America Press, 1951), 184–87.

14. *Calvin's New Testament Commentaries* 1:232; *John Calvin's Sermons on the Ten Commandments,* ed. and trans. Benjamin W. Farley (Grand Rapids: Baker Book House, 1980), 189.

15. Alan Donagan, *The Theory of Morality* (Chicago: University of Chicago Press, 1977), 59.

16. This is an appropriate place to note an important remark by Rosemary Radford Ruether about the role of women in the Gospel vision. "Among the poor it is the widows who are the most destitute. Among the ritually unclean, it is the woman with the flow of blood who exhorts healing for herself contrary to the law. Among the morally outcast, it is the prostitutes who are the furthest from righteousness. The role played by women of marginalized groups is an intrinsic part of the iconoclastic messianic vision. It means that the women are the oppressed of the oppressed" (*Sexism and God-Talk: Toward a Feminist Theology* [Boston: Beacon Press, 1983], 136).

17. Fitzmyer, *Gospel according to Luke I–IX,* 155.

18. Charles Curran, *Themes in Fundamental Moral Theology* (Notre Dame, Ind.: University of Notre Dame Press, 1977), 14–16.

19. H. Richard Niebuhr, "War as Crucifixion," *Christian Century* 60 (April 1943): 513–15.

20. *Calvin's New Testament Commentaries* 12:157.

21. Jack Dean Kingsbury, *Matthew: Structure, Christology, Kingdom* (Philadelphia: Fortress Press, 1975), 148–49.

22. Stanley Hauerwas, *The Peaceable Kingdom: A Primer in Christian Ethics* (Notre Dame, Ind.: University of Notre Dame Press, 1975), 77.

23. See Richard R. Niebuhr's "Archegos: An Essay on the Relation between the Biblical Jesus Christ and the Present–Day Reader," in *Christian History and Interpretation: Studies Presented to John Knox,* ed. W. R. Farmer, C. F. D. Moule, and R. R. Niebuhr (Cambridge: Cambridge University Press, 1967), 84, 87.

24. Wiles, *Faith and the Mystery of God,* 70–71.

25. Jonathan Edwards, "Treatise on Religious Affections," in *The Works of Jonathan Edwards,* memoir by Sereno E. Dwight, rev. Edward Hickman (Edinburgh: Banner of Truth Trust, 1974), 1:303–7.

26. Augustine, *The Enchiridion on Faith, Hope, and Love,* ed. Henry Paolucci (Chicago: Henry Regnery Co., 1961), 126; John Calvin, *The Institutes of the Christian Religion,* ed. John T. McNeill, trans. Ford Lewis Battles, vols. 20 and 21 of *The Library of Christian Classics* (Philadelphia: Westminster Press, 1960), 2.2.11.

27. Calvin, *Institutes* 3.7.1–5.

28. Edwards, "Dissertation on the Nature of True Virtue," *Works* 1:125–27; Edwards, *Charity and Its Fruits,* 176–77.

29. On the connection between love and self-denial see Edwards's *Charity and Its Fruits,* 235–36.

30. Charles M. Swezey, "Christian Self-Denial," *Journal for Preachers* 9, no. 2 (Lent 1986): 16.

31. R. R. Niebuhr, "Archegos," 91.

32. H. Richard Niebuhr, *Christ and Culture* (New York: Harper & Row, 1975), 28–29.

33. H. Richard Niebuhr, *Radical Monotheism and Western Culture with Supplementary Essays* (New York: Harper Torchbooks, 1970), 121.

34. Augustine, *The Enchiridion on Faith, Hope, and Love,* 38–39; idem, "Homilies on 1 John," 344.

35. Edwards, "Treatise on Religious Affections," 266, 274–75.

36. Calvin, *Institutes* 3.1.1–2.

37. Reinhold Niebuhr, *The Nature and Destiny of Man* (New York: Charles Scribner's Sons, 1943), 2:16ff.

38. H. Richard Niebuhr, "War as Crucifixion," 513–15.

39. Josiah Royce, *The Problem of Christianity* (Chicago: University of Chicago Press, 1968), 167.

40. Reinhold Niebuhr, *The Nature and Destiny of Man* 2:61.

41. Wiles, *Faith and the Mystery of God,* 58, 69.
42. Friedrich Schleiermacher, *The Christian Faith,* ed. H. R. Mackintosh and J. S. Stewart (Philadelphia: Fortress Press, 1976), §§69–72; Walter Rauschenbusch, *A Theology of the Social Gospel,* (Nashville: Abingdon Press, 1945), 93.
43. On interaction between emotional constitutions and social conditions, see Mary Midgley, *Beast and Man: The Roots of Human Nature* (Ithaca, N.Y.: Cornell University Press, 1978), 321–63, and Chapter Three above.
44. Schleiermacher, *The Christian Faith,* §71.
45. H. Richard Niebuhr, "War as Crucifixion," 513–15.
46. Gustaf Wingren, *Credo: The Christian View of Faith and Life* (Minneapolis: Augsburg, 1981), 81, 111.
47. On the transformative power of unearned suffering, see *A Testament of Hope: The Essential Writings of Martin Luther King, Jr.,* ed. James M. Washington (San Francisco: Harper & Row, 1986), 18, 41–42.
48. Eugene R. Fairweather, ed., *A Scholastic Miscellany: Anslem to Ockham* (New York: Macmillan Co., 1970), 176-79; Gustav Aulén claims that Luther also rejected the emphasis on penance and law characteristic of what Aulén calls "the Latin doctrine." See *Christus Victor: An Historical Study of the Three Main Types of the Idea of Atonement,* trans. A. G. Hebert (New York: Macmillan Co., 1969), 120–21.
49. *A Scholastic Miscellany,* 278, 283–84.
50. Aulén, *Christus Victor,* 120; Jaroslav Pelikan, *The Reformation of Church and Dogma 1300–1700,* vol. 4 of *The Christian Tradition* (Chicago: University of Chicago Press, 1984), 4:162–63. I return to this theme when I discuss the question of Christ's sinlessness in Chapter Five.
51. Horace Bushnell, *The Vicarious Sacrifice; Grounded in Principles Interpreted by Human Analogies* (New York: Charles Scribner's Sons, 1907), 1:105–26. The notion that we share Christ's sufferings is also present in the New Testament, for example 2 Corinthians and Phil. 3:10, and in early Christian literature, for example *The Martyrdom of Polycarp, Bishop of Smyrna.*
52. Sidney E. Ahlstrom, *A Religious History of the American People* (New Haven: Yale University Press, 1972), 686.
53. Martin Luther, *Theses for the Heidelberg Disputation,* no. 21.
54. I am aware, of course, that the righteous then answer with a question, "Lord, when did we see thee . . . ?" But the point cannot be that those who follow Jesus in the way should not recognize Jesus among those in need, else the saying itself lets the cat out of the bag. See also *Calvin's New Testament Commentaries* 3:116, on Matt. 25:37. Besides, when the unrighteous are confronted with their refusals to help those in need, they also ask, "Lord, when did we see thee . . . ?" So part of the point of the passage is to force a question of discernment.
55. Gustavo Gutiérrez, *A Theology of Liberation: History, Politics, and Salvation,*

ed. and trans. Sister Caridad Indo and John Eagleson (Maryknoll, N.Y.: Orbis Books, 1973), 200.

56. *Calvin's New Testament Commentaries* 3:116–17.

57. Joseph Sittler, *The Structure of Christian Ethics* (Baton Rouge: Louisiana State University Press, 1958), 24–64.

58. Reinhold Niebuhr, *Essays in Applied Christianity,* ed. D. B. Robertson (New York: World Publishing, Meridian Books, 1959), 29.

59. Barth, *Church Dogmatics* 3/2:448ff.

60. Emil Brunner, *The Christian Doctrine of Creation and Redemption,* vol. 2 of *Dogmatics,* trans. Olive Wyon (Philadelphia: Westminster Press, 1952), 371–72.

61. Similar points might be made also about the ascension. Again, the New Testament presents us with a variety of references, some more inclined toward a kind of tangible and visual imagery than others. See T. Hartley Hall 4th, "The Right Hand of God," *Journal for Preachers* 8, no. 3 (Easter 1985): 21–25.

62. Willi Marxsen, *The Resurrection of Jesus of Nazareth,* trans. Margaret Kohl (Philadelphia: Fortress Press, 1970), 138–41.

63. Peter Hodgson, *Jesus—Word and Presence: An Essay in Christology* (Philadelphia: Fortress Press, 1971), 231–32.

5. THE MEDIATOR

1. George A. Lindbeck (*The Nature of Doctrine: Religion and Theology in a Postliberal Age* [Philadelphia: Westminster Press, 1984], 85) claims that, when Nicea and Chalcedon are regarded as paradigms, "there may . . . be complete faithfulness to classical Trinitarianism and christology even when the imagery and language of Nicea and Chalcedon have disappeared from the theology and ordinary worship, preaching, and devotion."

2. D. M. Baillie, *God Was in Christ: An Essay on Incarnation and Atonement* (New York: Charles Scribner's Sons, 1948), 114.

3. Ibid., 130–31. The emphasis is Baillie's.

4. Augustine, *The Enchiridion on Faith, Hope, and Love,* ed. Henry Paolucci (Chicago: Henry Regnery Co., 1961), 39.

5. Jonathan Edwards, "A Treatise Concerning Religious Affections," in *The Works of Jonathan Edwards,* memoir by Sereno E. Dwight, rev. Edward Hickman (Edinburgh: Banner of Truth Trust, 1974), 1:236.

6. John Calvin, *The Institutes of the Christian Religion,* ed. John T. McNeill, trans. Ford Lewis Battles, vols. 20 and 21 of *The Library of Christian Classics* (Philadelphia: Westminster Press, 1960), 3.2.8.

7. Richard R. Niebuhr, *Experiential Religion* (New York: Harper & Row, 1972), 46.

8. See Mary Midgley's *Beast and Man: The Roots of Human Nature* (Ithaca, N.Y.: Cornell University Press, 1978), 54, 326–31.

9. Augustine, *De praedest. sanct* 1.15. Cited by Baillie, *God Was in Christ,* 118.

10. Richard R. Niebuhr, *Experiential Religion,* 124, 130.

11. Ibid., 119.

12. John E. Smith, *Experience and God* (New York and London: Oxford University Press, 1968), 79. The emphasis is Smith's.

13. Karl Barth, *Church Dogmatics,* trans. G. W. Bromiley et al., ed. G. W. Bromiley and T. F. Torrance (Edinburgh: T. & T. Clark, 1961), 4/1: 631ff.; 4/3.2: 647ff.; idem, *The Humanity of God* (Atlanta: John Knox Press, 1960), 48.

14. For a note on the development of trinitarian doctrine, see "Appendix. The Historical Development of Trinitarian Doctrine," following Chapter Six.

15. This line of thinking might support the contention that both Schleiermacher and Barth are right to treat the Trinity where they do. Schleiermacher, who has been almost willfully misread by some on this point, is correct to place the Trinity at the culmination of his dogmatics because that symbol represents a summary of the distinctive apprehension of God distributed throughout the whole of the experience of the Christian community. Barth is correct to place the Trinity near the beginning of his dogmatics because that symbol tells us where to look for the responsive power and presence of God.

16. I am in approximate agreement with the following statement by Joseph S. O'Leary (*Questioning Back: The Overcoming of Metaphysics in Christian Tradition* [Minneapolis: Winston Press, 1985], 217–18): "It seems that our faith is unable to transcend the naming of Father, Son, and Spirit towards its ontological ground. For us they indicate dimensions of the phenomenality of God in revelation; the terms 'substance' and 'person,' and even the language of divine 'relations,' seems an unnecessary redoubling of faith's naming of God, which distracts from the exploration of the phenomenality of which is thus named. The unity of God is not effectively preserved by the declaration that there is one underlying substance behind the three names, but should be sought instead in the interplay of the three dimensions in the experience of revelation."

17. Maurice Wiles, *The Making of Christian Doctrine* (London: Cambridge University Press, 1967), 176–77.

18. Augustine, *On the Trinity,* trans. Arthur W. Haddan, in volume 3 of *A Select Library of the Nicene and Post Nicene Fathers of the Christian Church,* ed. Philip Schaff (Grand Rapids: Wm. B. Eerdmans, 1956), 109.

19. Calvin, *Institutes* 1.13.5.

20. Ibid., 1.13.21. Nor is it the case that a reverent agnosticism respecting knowledge of God *a se* will encourage equally speculative, heretical affirmations that threaten the distinctive, multidimensional apprehension of God within the Christian community. It simply will not do to object that speculative reticence prevents us from smoking out Sabellians. For the

doctrine that God's very self is without distinctions and relations also is too speculative. Besides, there are other, more positive grounds on which to object to modalistic qualifications of the symbol of the monad when it is used to interpret our experience of God in space and time. See "Appendix. The Historical Development of Trinitarian Doctrine," following Chapter Six.

21. H. Richard Niebuhr, *Radical Monotheism and Western Culture with Supplementary Essays* (New York: Harper & Row, 1970), 39–42.

22. See Calvin, *Institutes* 4.17; Gerrish, *The Old Protestantism and the New: Essays on the Reformation Heritage* (Chicago: University of Chicago Press, 1982), 106–7.

23. There is, of course, a sense in which the *Logos* image as it is used in the Prologue to the Gospel of John refers to preexistent Wisdom becoming flesh, and on my interpretation of the mystery of Jesus Christ this is best regarded as something other than a literal or univocal statement. The Prologue itself is highly poetic literature, perhaps even a hymn adopted by the evangelist, and in it "there is not the slightest indication of interest in metaphysical speculations about relationships within God or in what later theology would call Trinitarian processions." Raymond E. Brown, *The Gospel of John I–XII,* in *The Anchor Bible* (Garden City, N.Y.: Doubleday & Co., 1966), xii–xxv, 23–24, 524.

24. Eugene R. Fairweather, ed., *A Scholastic Miscellany: Anselm to Ockham* (New York: Macmillan Co., 1970), 122–25, 134–36.

25. Ibid., 112–15, 118–19.

26. Ibid., 119.

27. Ibid., 138.

28. Ibid., 156–58.

29. I think this aligns me with those who affirm that the Word became fallen human nature. In a sermon, Edwards writes, "He did not take the human nature on him in its first, most perfect and vigorous state, but in that feeble forlorn state which it is in since the fall . . . ," *Works* 2:866. See also Barth, *Church Dogmatics* 1/2:167ff.

30. Reinhold Niebuhr, *The Nature and Destiny of Man* (New York: Charles Scribner's Sons, 1943), 2:73.

31. Claude Welch, *The Reality of the Church* (New York: Charles Scribner's Sons, 1958), 82–84.

6. THE CHRISTIAN WAY

1. Gustavo Gutiérrez, *We Drink from Our Own Wells: The Spiritual Journey of a People,* trans. Matthew J. O'Connell (Maryknoll, N.Y.: Orbis Books, 1984), 80–83.

2. James M. Gustafson, *Can Ethics Be Christian?* (Chicago: University of Chicago Press, 1975), 164.

3. H. Richard Niebuhr, *The Responsible Self: An Essay in Christian Moral Philosophy* (New York: Harper & Row, 1963), 154–56.
4. Max Weber, *The Sociology of Religion*, trans. Ephraim Fischoff, intro. by Talcott Parsons (Boston: Beacon Press, 1963), xxxi–xxxiii, 43–44, 60–65, 151–65.
5. Ibid., xxxvii–xxxviii, 67–69.
6. Richard R. Niebuhr, *Experiential Religion* (New York: Harper & Row, 1972), 112–13.
7. See George A. Lindbeck, *The Nature of Christian Doctrine: Religion and Theology in a Postliberal Age* (Philadelphia: Westminster Press, 1984), 30–39, 117–24; Stanley Hauerwas, *A Community of Character: Toward a Constructive Christian Social Ethic* (Notre Dame, Ind.: University of Notre Dame Press, 1981), 53–55; Edward Schillebeeckx, *The Understanding of Faith: Interpretation and Criticism* (New York: Seabury Press, 1974), 61.
8. James M. Gustafson, *Ethics from a Theocentric Perspective* (Chicago: University of Chicago Press, 1981), 1:196–97.
9. Max Weber, *The Sociology of Religion*, 68.
10. Mary Midgley, *Beast and Man: The Roots of Human Nature* (Ithaca, N.Y.: Cornell University Press, 1978), 285–317.
11. *Saint Augustine: Treatises on Various Subjects*, trans. Sister Mary Sarah Muldowney, R.S.M. et al., vol. 14 of *The Fathers of the Church* (Washington, D.C.: Catholic University of America Press, 1952), 238.
12. *Saint Augustine: The Catholic and Manichean Ways of Life*, trans. Donald A. Gallagher and Idella J. Gallagher, vol. 56 of *The Fathers of the Church* (Washington, D.C.: Catholic University of America Press, 1966), 22–23.
13. Augustine, *The City of God*, trans. Marcus Dods (New York: Random House, 1950), 158–71. H. Richard Niebuhr makes a similar argument about commonalities between radical devotion to God and certain loyalties among members of political and scientific communities in *Radical Monotheism and Western Culture* (New York: Harper & Row, 1970), 64–89.
14. Thomas Aquinas, *Summa Theologiae*, trans. Fathers of the Dominican Province (New York: Benziger Brothers, n.d.), 1–2, 100.
15. *Calvin's Sermons on the Ten Commandments*, trans. and ed. Benjamin W. Farley (Grand Rapids: Baker Book House, 1980), 133, 153, 189.
16. Arthur J. Dyck, *On Human Care: An Introduction to Ethics* (Nashville: Abingdon Press, 1977), 98–99.
17. James M. Gustafson, *Can Ethics Be Christian?*, 158.
18. Robert M. Grant, *Gnosticism and Early Christianity*, rev. ed. (New York: Harper Torchbooks, 1966), 1–38, 199–200.
19. *Saint Augustine: The Catholic and Manichean Ways of Life*, 109–10.
20. Gustafson argues that what is authorized theologically in Christian ethics cannot be converted without remainder into other forms of ethics (*Can Ethics Be Christian?*, 164–79).

21. Dietrich Bonhoeffer, *Letters and Papers from Prison,* ed. Eberhard Bethge, enlarged ed. (New York: Macmillan Co., 1971), 361–62.

22. See, for example, Erik H. Erikson, *Insight and Responsibility* (New York: Harper & Row, 1967), 109–57.

23. Claims like these about certain human predispositions are made by a number of writers. For example, Charles Darwin, *The Descent of Man, and Selection in Relation to Sex* (Princeton: Princeton University Press, 1981), 70–106; Midgley, *Beast and Man,* 58, 70, 333–41; Joseph Lopreato, *Human Nature and Biocultural Evolution* (Boston: Allen & Unwin, 1984), 335.

24. Obviously, there are many respects in which my interpretation might be opposed by followers of Barth. But is it really as entirely anti-Barthian as it appears? "To have experience of God's Word is to yield to its supremacy. Whether it comes to us as Law or Gospel, as command or promise, it comes at any rate in such a way as to bend man, and indeed his conscience and will no less than his intellect and feeling. It does not break him; it really bends him, brings him into conformity with itself." Karl Barth, *Church Dogmatics,* trans. G. W. Bromiley et al., ed. G. W. Bromiley and T. F. Torrance (Edinburgh: T. & T. Clark, 1975), 1/1:206.

25. Gustafson, *Can Ethics Be Christian?,* 64.

26. James M. Gustafson, "The Sectarian Temptation: Reflections on Theology, the Church and the University," *Proceedings of the Catholic Theological Society* 40 (1985): 83–94.

27. My remarks here are meant to outline general tendencies in recent theology and theological ethics rather than to engage in detailed analysis of specific individuals. Roughly, but only roughly, the first isolationist option approximates John Howard Yoder's position in *The Priestly Kingdom: Social Ethics as Gospel* (Notre Dame, Ind.: University of Notre Dame Press, 1984), 11, 40–41. The second approximates Lindbeck, *The Nature of Christian Doctrine,* 30–45, 112–35. The last, which is quite similar to the second, approximates Paul Holmer's position in a number of articles and *The Grammar of Faith* (New York: Harper & Row, 1978).

28. Douglas F. Ottati, *Meaning and Method in H. Richard Niebuhr's Theology* (Washington, D.C.: University Press of America, 1982), 1–11, 183–88; idem, "Christian Theology and Other Disciplines," *Journal of Religion* 64, no. 2 (April 1984): 173–87.

29. This position is compatible with the notion that there are multiple sources or reference points for Christian theology and ethics. See Lisa Sowle Cahill, *Between the Sexes: Foundations for a Christian Ethics of Sexuality* (Philadelphia: Fortress Press; Paramus, N.J.: Paulist Press, 1985), 4–11.

30. Ottati, "Christian Theology," 181.

31. Bonhoeffer's statement is in *Ethics,* ed. Eberhard Bethge (New York: Macmillan Co., 1955), 195. Here, however, I have revised an alternative

translation by Charles West, *Communism and the Theologians* (Philadelphia: Westminster Press, 1958), 344. Also cited in James M. Gustafson, *Christ and the Moral Life* (Chicago: University of Chicago Press, 1976), 32, Bonhoeffer's statement is as follows: "The Reality of God discloses itself only by setting me entirely in the reality of the world; but there I find the reality of the world always already sustained, accepted, and reconciled in the reality of God."

32. Edward Farley, *Theologia: The Fragmentation and Unity of Theological Education* (Philadelphia: Fortress Press, 1983), 8–9.

33. Conrad Cherry, *Nature and Religious Imagination: From Edwards to Bushnell* (Philadelphia: Fortress Press, 1980), 26–31.

34. Jonathan Edwards, *Scientific and Philosophical Writings,* vol. 6 of *Works of Jonathan Edwards,* ed. Wallace E. Anderson (New Haven: Yale University Press, 1980), 397.

35. See, for example, Wilfred Cantwell Smith, *Towards a World Theology* (Philadelphia: Westminster Press, 1981), 152–79.

36. David Tracy writes that "we understand one another, if at all, only through analogies," (*The Analogical Imagination: Christian Theology and the Culture of Pluralism* [New York: Crossroads, 1981], 363). Gordon D. Kaufman, (*The Theological Imagination: Constructing the Concept of God* [Philadelphia: Westminster Press, 1981], 118, 168, 198), claims that specifications of what is authentically human in Christ may be generalized to serve as significant points for dialogue.

37. See Helder Camara's "What Would St. Thomas Aquinas, the Aristotle Commentator, Do if Faced with Karl Marx?" in *Celebrating the Medieval Heritage: A Colloquy on the Thought of Aquinas and Bonaventure,* ed. David Tracy, *Journal of Religion* 58, supp. (1978): 174–82.

38. H. Richard Niebuhr, *The Meaning of Revelation* (New York: Macmillan Co., 1941), 139.

APPENDIX: THE HISTORICAL DEVELOPMENT OF TRINITARIAN DOCTRINE

1. J. N. D. Kelly, *Early Christian Doctrines,* 2d ed. (New York: Harper & Row, 1960), 110–15, 126–32; Origen, *On First Principles,* trans. G. W. Butterworth (Gloucester, Mass.: Peter Smith, 1975), 2–3, 10, 15–16, 30, 33–34.

2. What is called "dynamic monarchianism" in the textbooks is a different teaching that combined strict monotheism with adoptionist christologies. This earlier development does not directly concern us here. See Reinhold Seeberg, *Text-book of the History of Doctrines,* trans. Charles E. Hay (Grand Rapids: Baker Book House, 1958), 1:162; Kelly, *Doctrines,* 115–19.

3. Saint Basil writes as follows in his *Letters,* vol. 2 of *Fathers of the Church* (New York: Fathers of the Church, 1955), 31–33: "It is very necessary for

us to be guided in our investigations of the divine nature by its operations
. . . if we consider the operation of the Father and of the Son and of the
Holy Spirit to be one, differing or varying in no way at all, it is necessary
because of the identity of operation for the oneness of the nature to be
inferred. . . . He who infers that matters beyond us are administered by
the power of the Spirit with the Father and the Son affirms confidently
concerning these things, supported by a clear testimony accruing from
his own life." See also Kelly, *Doctrines,* 263–69; Maurice Wiles, *The Making
of Christian Doctrine* (Cambridge: Cambridge University Press, 1967), 128.
4. Kelly, *Doctrines,* 271–79.

Index